GLORIOUS GARDENS

of IRELAND

GLORIOUS GARDENS
of IRELAND

with a foreword by Jim Reynolds

MELANIE ECLARE

Kyle Cathie Limited

For Tom, with all my love

This book has been a big part of my life for a couple of years, during which time I have befriended many of the gardeners. Without their support and help this book would not have been possible – it wasn't easy, but they made my travels delightful, welcoming me with warmth and generosity. I want to thank everyone who I came across along the way, for guiding and encouraging me.

Jim Reynolds

Jim Reynolds

BUTTERSTREAM

ON AN OLD FLOODPLAIN OF THE RIVER BOYNE IN THE HEART OF THE IRISH MIDLANDS, Butterstream garden is tucked away behind tall hedging on the suburban outskirts of Trim, Co. Meath. In contrast to the popular image of Irish gardens as lush, semi-tropical paradises, the climate here is variable, liable to harsh frosts and severe wind with soil of heavy limestone and clay. Ignoring all these factors, owner Jim Reynolds has gradually extended his garden, from a small rose garden to a contemporary vision of arcadia. He declares that his passion for gardening came 'like a rush of blood to the head,' when he was a student at Trinity College, Dublin, and over twenty years he has designed and planted a complex and maze-like series of connecting garden compartments stretching over one and three quarter hectares (four acres) of what was once the family farm.

The garden has been cleverly created to hide the house beyond the hedging and shut out the surrounding suburban landscape. Jim delights in this secrecy which adds to the magical otherworldly atmosphere of his garden. As you move though the garden each separate room claims its own particular mood through its structure, form and colour, constantly changing as you are compelled onwards with the sight of an urn, gate or pavilion.

The design is led by architectural follies and relics such as the Gothic wooden bridge that leads across the stream into

PREVIOUS LEFT
Jim Reynolds in front of
the herbaceous
borders, with the
viewing tower in the
backround.

PREVIOUS RIGHT
A winter's view across the
garden, past the fastigiate
yews to the pavilions.

LEFT   View across the
lawn to the Yew Walk and
Medusa fountain through
copper beech hedging.

RIGHT   The same view
through the copper beech
archway in the winter.

the first woodland area; the high boundaries are native hedging of beech and ash.

The first time I arrived at Butterstream, in the heatwave of 1995, I was travelling around Ireland photographing gardens on a Merlin Trust scholarship. Turning up at six in the evening I ran through the garden looking for Jim. Getting lost in the long dark corridors of high beech, I felt like Alice in Wonderland as the garden opened out in front of me and I found myself in a huge circular dreamscape with 6m (20ft) deep herbaceous borders brimming with giant flowers. Huge

spires of deep blue aconitums and *Campanula lactiflora* blended with the vibrant purple loosestrife *Lythrum salicaria* and the burning bush *Dictamnus* var. *purpureus*. If you can, it is worth driving a long way to see these borders at their peak during June, July and August.

The irregular shape of the garden means that it falls naturally into a series of distinct areas. Crossing the Gothic bridge, the shady woodland garden is reached with damp shade-loving primulas, blue meconopsis poppies, ferns, astilbes and hostas growing beneath the arching *Rosa moyesii* with its scarlet single flowers and long drooping red hips. Jim

confesses to once being a victim of hosta-fever, even crossing the Atlantic in search of new and unusual varieties including the slow-growing *H. tokudama*, with its puckered glaucous deep blue-green leaves.

Beyond a rose garden, with old-fashioned varieties of roses, is the white garden. White forms of delphiniums, campanulas, sweet rocket, borage, agapanthus and thistles such as the grand *Onopordum acanthium* stand guard around an elegant viewing tower. 'Everyone insists on calling it my "Rapunzel Tower" after a journalist called it that, but it's not,' explains Jim. It is a copy of a local pigeon tower and

LEFT   A 1740s door surround from a Georgian house at the end of the main street in Trim, originally owned by Lord Longford.

RIGHT   The Roman pool garden was inspired by a trip to Pompeii. Clipped bays and lollipop box sit outside the loggia. The interior is painted Etruscan Red.

RIGHT BELOW The pink water lily *Nymphaea* 'Fire Crest' floats on the Roman pool.

designed as a viewing platform. Looking from the top of its external staircase across the upper garden you see how the rooms interconnect. Past the white garden below, a path leads across the herbaceous borders, through a weeping laburnum arch (shortly to be removed) to a gravel garden. This contains a group of yew incarcerated in trellis and pyramid-shaped box. Beyond is the formal Roman garden, begun after a trip to Pompeii. Its oblong pool, capped with soft grey Liscannor paving and lollipop box plants in terracotta pots, gives a feeling of calm and balance.

A romantic traditionalist at heart, Jim has gained many ideas from travels to Italy in recent years. A proficient cook

himself, he describes creating a garden as akin to giving a dinner party, providing different courses to excite or cool the palette. As each course is entirely distinct from the last, so every part of the garden aims to be complete in itself ranging from the wild to the formal, the sensual to the ordered. His garden's calming pauses between courses are the cool green corridors which lead to hot Mediterranean areas lividly coloured in bronzes and reds where ligularias like tall yellow fireworks, red tiger lilies and golden grasses prickle the light.

Jim's greatest indulgence to date lies at the farthest end of the garden. Behind the double archway of the portico relic and an echoing copper beech hedge, an expanse of courtyard sits centrally between two Georgian pavilions, grandly Italianate. Based on the Villa Lante, north of Rome, Jim designed the plans for the buildings and employed local craftsmen and builders to construct them. The style includes heavy cornices, Corinthian pilasters and Venetian windows. They took a year and a half to complete. As Jim recalls, 'I just walked up and down, pacing about at night to get the size right. But there'd be no fun if it didn't cause an awful lot of sweat. No cross, no crown.' This motto certainly rings true for his latest undertaking. Beyond the pavilions is another surprise. Two 40m (130ft) canals, worthy of Versailles, float away from either end of the pavilions, an avenue of limes flanking their length. Yet another breathtaking vision.

Indeed Jim Reynolds is an astonishing man who possesses the rare ability to make his own dreams reality and also to inspire others to do so. To support his own fervour for gardening and maintain the adrenalin rush of the new, Jim acts as garden consultant on projects around Ireland. He is often away, driving down to Kerry, Cork or Donegal in the early hours to 'fight with the contractors'. He is also

Chairman of the EC-funded body, The Great Gardens of Ireland Restoration Scheme, promoting the timely renaissance of Irish gardens, and Ireland's return to its late-nineteenth-century position as the garden of Europe. Jim's own garden houses a marvellous collection of Irish-named cultivars of primulas and other plants, many endangered, discovered on travels around the country in his previous job as an archaeologist.

Butterstream is one of Ireland's most popular gardens today and, if Jim keeps it developing as he promises, it will always remain so.When I ask him where he's going next, he immediately has the perfect reply 'We've got a long way to go yet' – quoting lines from his favourite Bob Dylan song, *Brown Town*, about a young girl hitching a lift. 'How far are you going?' she asks, 'Goin' all the way, until these wheels fall off and burn.'

FAR LEFT *Lythrum salicaria* is one of the native herbaceous plants Jim uses to great effect in his borders, planting in massed swathes.

LEFT *Veronica* 'Crater Blue Lake' and *Artemisia ludoviciana*, which runs riot in the border.

ABOVE Jim modelled his tower on a local ruined pigeon tower. The beds in front are 6m (20ft) deep, a mass of blues, whites, mauves and pinks all summer.

Keith Lamb

WOODFIELD

DEEP IN THE HEART OF THE BOGS IN CO. OFFALY, there lies a small garden which is both extremely important and very beautiful. Although occupying the relatively confined space around a handsome early eighteenth-century house, this garden is a plantsman's paradise, and evokes a sense of serenity, tranquility and peace. It belongs to Dr Keith Lamb, one of Ireland's most senior horticulturists.

LEFT   A path through the 'jungle' garden underplanted with hostas, bergenias, ferns and myosotidiums.

RIGHT   The garden includes a collection of unusual insect-eating North American pitcher plants, including this *Sarracenia purpurea*.

Following a degree in horticulture from University College, Dublin in 1948, Dr Lamb began his research at the Agricultural Institute in Wexford, and at the Horticultural Research Centre in Malahide where he studied the botany of vegetables, and latterly, hardy plants. Now he is retired and gardens for pleasure.

To the untrained eye, early glimpses of the garden are unpromising: a short avenue of beech trees which once lined the drive appear to stand alone until closer inspection reveals a magical woodland garden brimming with bulbs. 'People say you cannot grow things under beech trees,' he says, 'but this isn't so because there are many things that come up before their leaves are out.' On a late spring morning Dr Lamb points to the blue, yellow, white and double-white wood anemones, and the delicately arched young stems of Solomon's seal *Polygonatum x hybridum* with their drooping white flowers, and a rich carmine pink spring cyclamen *C. repandum*. 'It seeds itself,' he says, 'but it likes to be planted deep.' He concedes that in the height of summer the woodland floor is slightly bare but the autumn cyclamen are soon in their stride, and the cycle starts again in early spring with aconites and twelve different types of snowdrop.

Close by *Trillium sessile*, with extraordinary reddish brown flowers standing erect above a collar of three-lobed leaves,

has seeded freely into the limestone gravel in front of the house. The front door is framed by two deliciously sweet-scented daphnes, the evergreen *D. bholua* 'Jacqueline Postill' and the slower growing *D. bholua* var. *glaccalis* 'Gurkha'. Dr Lamb calls the latter 'a marvellous plant with a marvellous scent. It is deciduous, flowers before Christmas and with-stands the weather.' It seems that often troublesome daphnes present no problems here; Dr Lamb also has a fine specimen of *D. x burkwoodii* 'Somerset', which is unusually fast-growing ,with pale pink fragrant flowers in May and June.

It is at first surprising that despite the proximity of the acid bogs his garden is on limestone. This becomes less of a puzzle when you learn that the bogs were lakes in the Ice Age. As reeds, marsh plants and vegetation started to build up, they gradually lost the limestone influence. With increas-ing rainfall, plant residues turned acidic, and bogs gradually formed. The surrounding limestone stayed put allowing many lime-loving plants to thrive at Woodfield.

To the side of the house are numerous bulbs including chionodoxas with their pretty little blue star-shaped flowers, dogs' tooth lilies (erythroniums), purple fritillaries and the showy lady's slipper orchid *Cypripedium reginae* with its fat pink lip.

There is also a staggering number of rare alpine plants which Dr Lamb has obtained from collections all over the world. These include the pure blue Glasnevin form of *Gentiana loderi* and *Cyclamen libanoticum* which is now 'uncommon and rare in the wild'. He is also growing the

FAR LEFT *Viola cornuta* 'Boughton blue'.

FAR RIGHT Fern fronds thrive in the damp shade of the woodland garden.

LEFT The seed head of the rare *Pulsatilla* 'Budapest'.

Balearic natives *Cyclamen balearicum* and the tiny white Majorcan peony *Paeonia cambessedesii*.

In the old kennel yard behind the house seven lime-free raised beds have been constructed for some of the smaller alpines which might get overlooked in a bigger garden. One bed is devoted to insectivorous North American pitcher plants, sarracenias, that have naturalised in the surrounding bogs. Other plants such as the tiny *Primula muscarioides* appear next to a rare form of the monkey musk *Mimulus primuloides*. A Himalayan poppy *Meconopsis lancifolia* rubs shoulders with the yellow daisy *Inula rhizocephala*. It is anyone's guess what you might find here, but extremely unlikely that you will find the same plants in many other gardens.

Alpines play a large part in Dr Lamb's planting scheme, but there is another side to the garden, a larger world of trees, shrubs, foliage and shade. Dr Lamb explains 'It is an unplanned jungle. I plant where I can. And because it is away from the garden I do not cut off any dead stems, just let everything fall as in nature.'

A magical forest in miniature, it has plants in corresponding different layers, from the root zone up to the canopy. Myosotidiums, the Chatham Island forget-me-nots that grow so well in Ireland, join fleshy-leafed bergenias at ground level. Above them tower gunnera and rodgersias which are impaled by the giant spires of cardiocrinums and a magnificent clump of kirengeshomas. *Clematis montana* leads the eye upwards to the ancient oaks and limes that make up the canopy together with *Magnolia stellata*, birches, rowans and

the Judas tree *Cercis siliquastrum*. The paths are littered with plant debris making it spongy underfoot. The air is cool and the filtered light creates a magical atmosphere.

It is unexpected to discover such an untamed area in a serious collector's garden but it is this rare combination of horticultural plantsmanship and wild 'jungle' that makes this secret garden so intriguing.

FAR LEFT   A rare alpine *Zaluzianshya* 'Midnight Taylor' in one of Dr Lamb's raised beds.

ABOVE   The pink form of *Meconopsis napaulensis* in the woodland garden.

RIGHT   A magical damp space with dappled light filtering through the trees, in the 'jungle' garden. Plants are allowed to behave just as nature wishes.

Desmond & Olda Fitzgerald

GLIN CASTLE

GLIN CASTLE, THE HOME OF THE 27TH KNIGHT OF GLIN AND MADAM FITZGERALD, has been in the same family for over 600 years. Overlooking the majestic River Shannon in the north-west of Co. Limerick, this beautiful eighteenth-century castle comes straight from the pages of a fairy tale. Visitors are welcomed for dinner, over-night stays and breakfast.

The sheer romanticism and stunning position of Glin, as well as its high levels of comfort, attract visitors from all over the world. There are pleasure grounds to stroll in and a walled garden full of amazing delicacies that end up on the dining room table. The castle's proximity to the sea and the abundance of moisture in the air gives Glin the mild microclimate for which cold-climate gardeners often yearn.

From the front of the castle there is a dreamlike view north past follies standing watch, over the wide river to Co. Clare. The Shannon is 2km (over 1 mile) wide at this point just before it hits the Atlantic. The pleasure grounds spread out behind the castle and add to the feeling of wide open space. Stately trees in the grounds include blue cedars, limes and tall beech, but one outstanding tree, a lone Monterey pine *Pinus radiata,* stands even taller than the three-storey castle, and seems to dwarf the building.

In the shade of this tree a gravel path leads away from the castle, past a pair of bay trees *Laurus nobilis* clipped like ink-cap mushrooms, to a circle of yews enclosing a sundial. Walls behind are softened by ceanothus, wisteria and *Rosa* 'Felicité and Perpetue'.

A *Parrotia persica* lies right at the top of the walk. This is the perfect tree for such a position as it has three distinct phases – brown bracts with red stamens in the spring, strong green foliage in the summer turning to red and gold in the autumn. Either side of the walk the lawns are neatly manicured, their generous expanse of green like an extension of the river bank.

Beyond the parrotia and the low wall signifying the end of the formal garden, the land rises gently through a meadow to a wood on the brow of the hill. In the spring, naturalised in the grass, are masses of daffodils brought back from the gardens at Tresco on the Isles of Scilly. New plantings of large-leafed rhododendrons have been established at the top of the hill.

On the other side of the castle, the pleasure grounds are

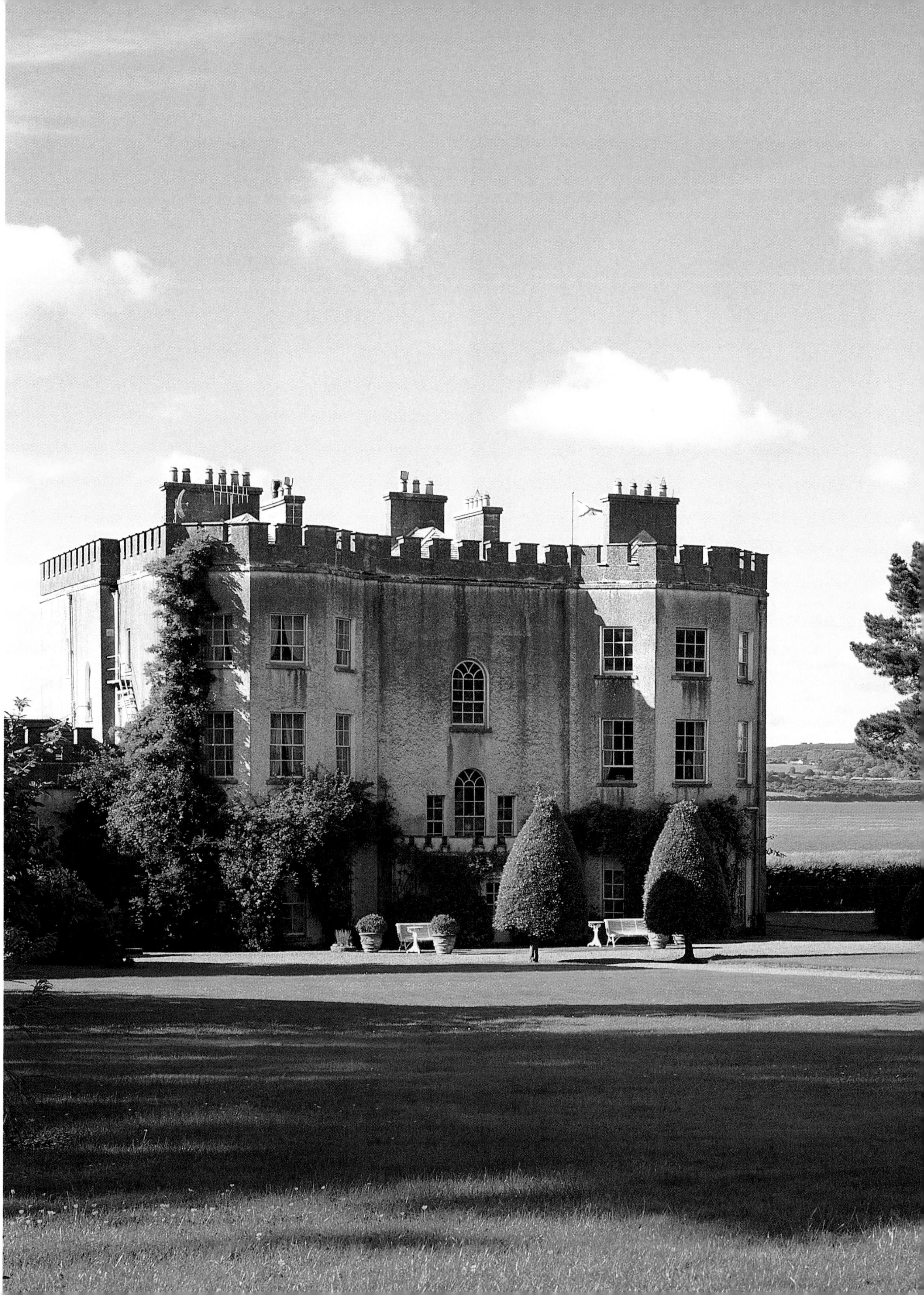

divided from the walled garden by a mature shrubbery. Planting here includes myrtles, hydrangeas and magnolias with camellias and a *Sophora tetraptera* planted by the Knight's mother in 1929, alongside a *Crinodendron hookeri-anum* and a tall fragrant *Drimys winteri*, planted by his grandmother in 1890. Speckles of peeling bark from a half hidden *Luma apiculata* become phosphorescent as the breeze carries them off.

A productive walled garden beyond the pleasure grounds needs constant attention. Fruit, vegetables, herbs and flowers are all grown here for the house under the experienced eye of gardener Tom Wall. Born 14km (9 miles) away but raised in Glin, Tom has worked for the Fitzgeralds for twenty-two years, twenty-one of those in the garden. Inside the 1 hectare (2 1/2 acre) plot he produces specialities for family and guests. The sea kale is highly popular and the asparagus, he says, 'is in such demand that we have had to put in a new bed.' Apples and soft fruit grow here, and the bottom border is devoted entirely to roses for cutting.

Annuals including sunflowers, sweet peas and cosmos are raised in the greenhouse, planted out as bedfellows to globe artichokes and majestic silver-leafed cardoons *Cynara cardun-culus* in the long, sloping borders. But along with the many regimented rows of peas and beans, chards and lettuces, the walled garden has its lighter side: the Gothic chicken house has its own castellated battlements.

Secreted in the woods behind the walled garden is the hermitage. Remnants of bamboo clumps show this is the site of an old garden. The low-slung, triple-arched folly was built in the last century to resemble the entrance to a vault. The cobbled floor and brick ceiling have remained in good order and the only recent additions are a stone seat, stone skull, and the initials of one John Dillon dated 4/5/1921.

Trees in front of the hermitage have been cleared to make room for an elegant circle of seven standing stones with a large central boulder. Through the trees the river can be glimpsed, sometimes bright blue, though more often grey and moody, serving as a reminder of all the history that has passed here and constantly adding an atmospheric touch to any visit to this solitary castle.

Rod Alston

EDEN PLANTS

'WE STARTED OUT AS A MAIL-ORDER BUSINESS SELLING HERBS in the mid-1970s, but then found to our astonishment that people would actually drive all the way here and back from Dublin. It seems they were curious to see what herb plants actually looked like. In the late 1970s we started to sell cut herbs to the restaurant trade but no-one was interested.'

This is how Rod Alston of Eden Plants near Rossinver, Co. Leitrim, remembers his early days of organic food production. Now the owner of a thriving business, Rod grows and sells herbs and vegetables under the symbol of the Organic Trust of Ireland.

Hidden up a narrow lane, the nursery is enclosed by high hedges of hawthorn and hazel. It backs on to the rolling Leitrim Hills and commands beautiful views over Lough Melvin to the heathered hillsides beyond.

Rod moved here in 1974 with what he describes as 'naive ideas about self-sufficiency and selling surpluses as they arose.' Although he soon realised that there was a lot more to it than he first imagined, many of his self-sufficiency ideas have remained: the holding still produces most of its own fuel and food including vegetables, fruit, milk, cheese, yoghurt and quark (a type of soft cheese). In true smallholding tradition even suckler calves are for sale.

When he took over the holding 'It was a very boggy bit of ground, covered in blackthorn and rushes. It had shallow topsoil, high in organic matter but very acidic, and underneath was impervious limestone. Once I'd removed the trees I dug the whole plot myself with a Fermanagh shovel using a variation of the lazy bed system used in the west of Ireland and Scotland. It took two and a half months, but there is no quicker method of cultivating ground by hand. You just turn the sod over, making maximum use of the topsoil, to create a mound which gives automatic drainage.'

LEFT   Small seedlings of valerian, waiting to be potted on in early summer.

ABOVE   Rows of broad beans and onions in the lower garden, with the Leitrim Hills in the distance.

BELOW   The herb nursery area where Rod sells potted herbs and unusual plants.

Rod's digging made it possible to create twenty-seven raised beds which form the basis of the nursery. They are 90cm (3ft) wide and vary in length, with a gap of 45cm (18 in) between beds so that all cultivation can be done from the path, 'saving the back and saving the bed'. Rod operates a simple four-course rotation and in winter the beds are mulched with manure.

Even before the herb business, the very first produce to come out of Eden was vegetables sold through a co-operative, The Leitrim Vegetable Growers Association still flourishes today selling through a local organic shop. Growers formally agree who will grow what each season, and they try to be sensitive to the needs of other small growers even if they are not members.

Then the herbs started to take off. The business began because Rod had been trying to buy a reasonable range of herbs to use 'but found that even the ordinary kinds were

unavailable, so we decided to grow them ourselves.' He tried to get chefs interested in taking Eden's herbs but in the early 1970s 'to no avail. That showed the state of food in this country.' So he and his partner decided, reluctantly, to operate through mail order because they did not think anyone would find their way to the nursery. 'Then the late Theodora Fitzgibbon, the cookery correspondent for the *Irish Times*, did a big piece on us and we have never had to advertise since. Now we get enquiries from fifteen to twenty restaurants every year, but only supply a few who take more and more each year.'

Salads make up the largest part of the outdoor crops grown at Eden. Rod grows a wide range of lettuces including 'Lolla Rossa' and 'Lolla Bionda', 'Till' a German butterhead type, 'Catalogna', red and green 'Oak Leaf', the Swiss 'Trotzkopf', and a red butterhead 'Boston Burgundy'. Endive, frisée and radicchio are grown for late-season use. Other out-

FAR LEFT A view across the main garden of raised beds.

LEFT Courgette plants and celery in one of the polytunnels.

RIGHT Khaki Campbell ducks are on permanent patrol to keep slugs and snails down.

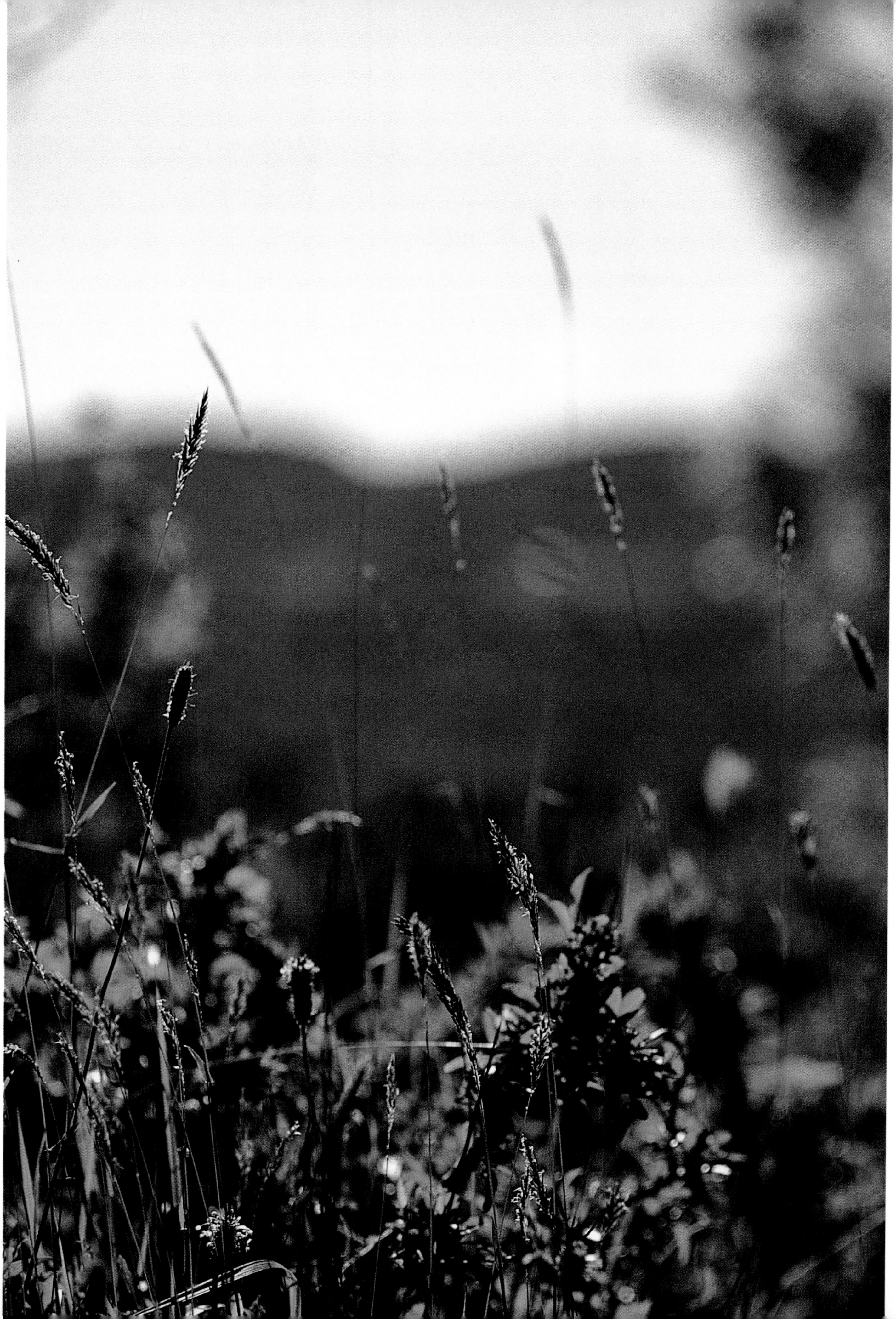

side crops include scallions or bunching onions, ruby chard, summer purslane, potatoes and herbs. Seven polythene tunnels give year-long produce.

Rod says, 'Since we have a small plot with only two acres, our crops have to be of high value.' Basil features prominently, along with coriander, dill, fennel and tarragon. There are also courgettes, tomatoes, aubergines, climbing French beans and sweet corn. Radishes, salad rocket and mizuna greens make up much of the winter crops.

Many of the stock plants for the herb nursery are grown here too including bay, marjoram and thymes, their blue flowers covered in bees which help pollinate the tomatoes. Poached egg plants *Limnanthes douglasii* spread out at the mouths of the tunnels attracting parasitic wasps and hoverflies to protect the main crops from aphids.

In addition to his work on the holding, Rod finds time to sit on the Board of the Organic Centre, just down the road. Established to meet the growing demand for information on organic gardening and farming, in Ireland, the centre has been open to the public since 1997. It provides technical assistance on all aspects organic through its demonstration gardens and runs year-round courses on a range of subjects from herb and organic kitchen gardening to beekeeping. Rod teaches at the Organic centre.

Eden Plants is a paradigm of self-sufficiency and organic food production. Raised beds are a rich dark colour and crops are healthy and vigorous. You'd think the luscious plants would be a mecca for pigeons but Rod has no trouble from them. Why? 'Because I'll be up at dawn and still working at ten at night.' Eden Plants is ordered, harmonious and successful, simply through Rod's dedication and hard work.

Janie Metcalfe
OLD FARM

JANIE METCALFE IS HAPPY TO ADMIT THAT SHE HAD NEVER GARDENED IN HER LIFE before 1981, nor

had she any interest in doing so. But that was the year when she and her husband Brian drove up the

Jericho Road a few miles from Killyleagh in Co. Down and bought Old Farm. 'It was pouring with

rain and all we could see from the top of a south-facing drumlin was a wilderness'.

The Metcalfes were looking for a farmhouse to restore and a few acres of land on which to keep their horses. After a long search they settled on this 18 hectare (45 acre) site though there was only a burnt-out ruin and a collection of old farm buildings dormant under a head-high blanket of bramble, ivy, nettle and thistle. 'It was' says Janie, 'like a time capsule of a place, unchanged since it was laid out in 1800, quietly disappearing back into the land. This was to be our garden'. It was several years later, after the house had been completed and yard buildings roofed, doored and shuttered, that the first tentative steps were taken towards tackling the planting.

LEFT *Geranium pratense* self-seeds and cross breeds with other geraniums such as the stripey *G.* 'Mrs Kendall-Clarke' to produce seedlings whose flowers can be anything from slate grey to deep azure blue, or a stripey combination of the two.

ABOVE Janie allows everything in the gravel garden to self-seed. Armenian cranesbill *Geranium psilostemon, G. renardii*, blue alpine aquilegias, toadflax and poppies thrive here.

LEFT Vigorous *Rosa* 'Paul's Himalayan Musk' clambers through the arch to the paddock. Janie built the arch with her husband Brian. Finding the right stones from the surrounding land turned the project into a lengthy ordeal.

RIGHT The rich mauve *Papaver orientale* 'Patty's plum' came from a plant sale at Castle Ward in Co. Down.

FAR RIGHT Janie's home-made coldframe with self-seeded white foxgloves and *Lychnis coronaria* 'Dancing Ladies' which is white with a pink eye.

Eighteen years on, the garden is a triumph of design and plantsmanship. All this has been achieved despite the difficulties of the soil and the weather conditions. The prevailing winds give an even rainfall of about 100cm (36in) a year, but although Strangford Lough is barely a quick jog away to the east and the sea not much further beyond, frosts are not kept at bay. Janie calls the soil 'poor, thin and sharply draining, with at best a thin layer of topsoil over shale, rock and boulder.' A pickaxe and crowbar are essential tools for making holes for trees and shrubs, even for herbaceous preparation, 'followed by digging in as much organic matter as possible. It is a very laborious process.'

'I read somewhere,' Janie adds, 'that one should "take out" a hole rather than dig it. But once you've taken out a hole here and removed the stones there is never enough soil to refill it.' This means that everything gets kick-started with copious quantities of manure.

The first plantings were designed to clothe the nakedness of the newly finished house. On Boxing Day 1988 Janie's roses 'New Dawn', 'Alberic Barbier', 'Wedding Day' and 'Handel' were all planted with bucketfuls of manure. She had no idea that those first cautious plantings would lead to the cultivation of the courtyard, the old stackyard and the paddock, and the construction of a greenhouse from the old henhouse. It is here Janie nurtures cuttings of tender plants such as her salvias S. *cacaliifolia*, S. 'Indigo Spire' and S. *fulgens* which look like red Turkish slippers.

Janie talks of her garden lovingly but with a stoic recognition that problems will keep arising. One of her biggest current worries is the presence of the New Zealand flatworm which has eaten all the common earthworms in the garden and hampered her attempts to improve the thin soil. On top of this they are plagued with rabbits. Yet the garden looks remarkably healthy.

LEFT   The rose 'Buff Beauty' entwines itself through *Iris siberica*.

RIGHT   The view across the paddock garden to a single ash tree and hawthorn hedges planted into stonefaced banks (the local method of hedging over drumlin country). Wildflowers such as oxeye daisies, poppies and meadow cranesbill here are completely naturalised.

Janie sticks to the plants that she has learned, through experience, can cope with the conditions. 'I am a self-confessed plantaholic, there is so much I would like to grow. But anything which needs deep soil and moisture, or shelter, is going to look miserable and make me feel terribly sad.'

She adds, 'A great gardening friend, Yvonne, fortunately got me started with clumps of several of the toughest and most resilient varieties of hardy geraniums. I now have about thirty different kinds from dainty gravel lovers including the tiny, clump-forming *Geranium cinereum* 'Ballerina', through to gobsmackers like the vermilion *G.* 'Ann Folkard' which sprawls and climbs through the other plants. They thrive in the dry soil.' Janie also loves penstemons, because they flower for such a long time and so late into the autumn. She has about twenty-eight varieties and takes cuttings so that she can renew them every two or three years.

The other great survivors here are the self-seeders, such as *Verbena bonariensis* whose small purple flowerheads reach up on long thin stems. Another tall favourite is the evening primrose *Oenothera stricta* 'Sulphurea'. Her design skills have been honed by a course in 1998 at the John Brooks school of garden design in Sussex.

Janie's garden is defined by the old stone walls and buildings. It has evolved to follow the lie of the land. There is not a straight line in the place. All the planting that has been done over the last ten years is suddenly starting to look established, and the walls of the old buildings, so assiduously cleared of ivy all those years ago, have virtually disappeared under layers of clematis, honeysuckle, wisteria and roses. Janie thinks that the garden is best described as 'barely controlled chaos', then adds 'I still have the feeling that were I to turn my back for too long, nature would quickly reclaim it as her own – but I don't intend to give her the chance.'

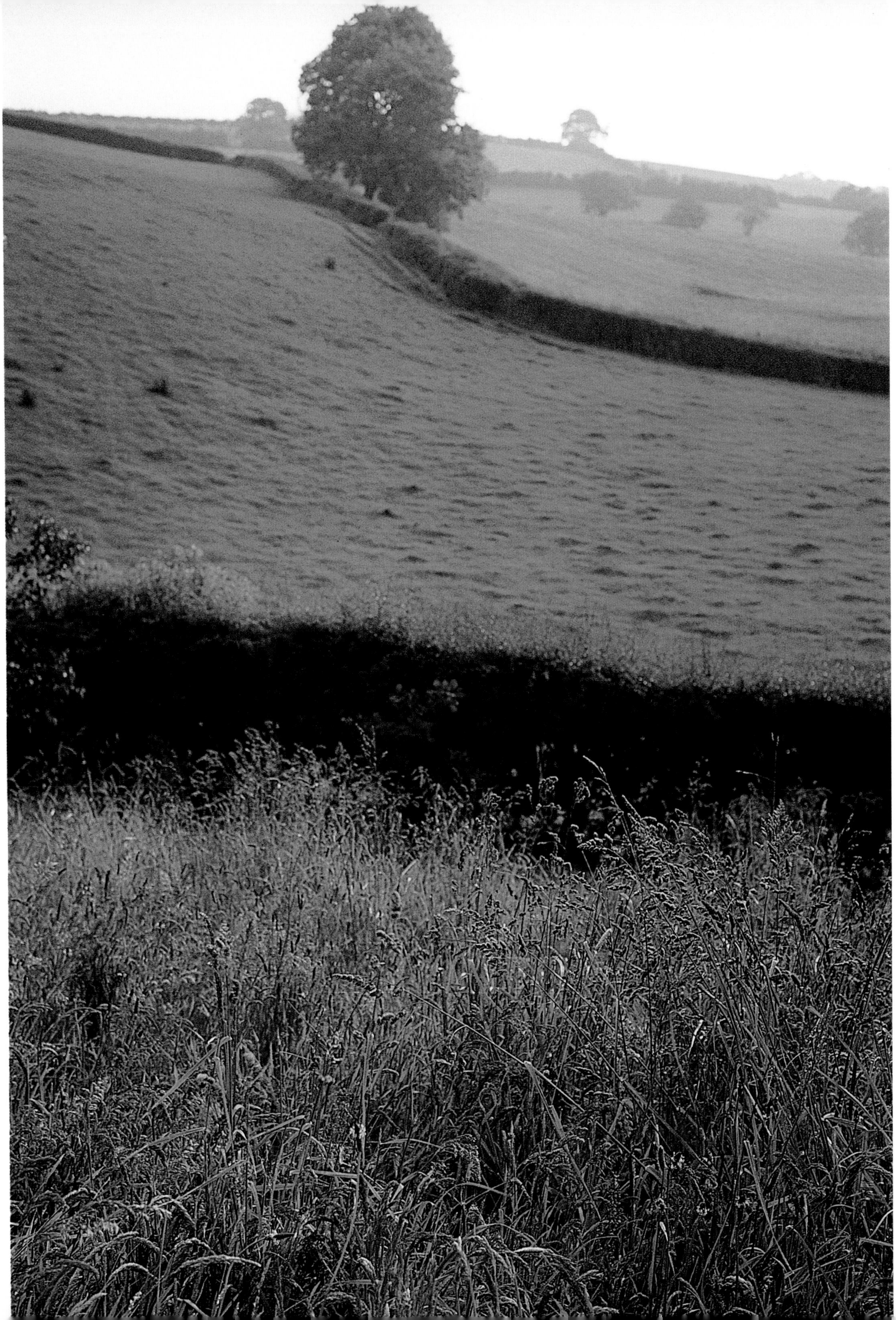

National Trust
MOUNT STEWART

ON THE EASTERNMOST POINT OF THE ARDS PENINSULA IN CO. DOWN, warmed by the Gulf Stream and close to Strangford Lough, lies Mount Stewart. Regarded today as one of the greatest gardens in Europe, it was created by the late Marchioness of Londonderry in the early 1920s. Mount Stewart is original and radically different from most gardens, awe-inspiring not so much for its size nor for the scale of its grandeur, but because of its style and content, wit and subtlety. It reflects a life of politics, society, history, travel and high culture. The 32 hectare (80 acre) garden that exists today has been in the hands of The National Trust since 1955.

When Lady Londonderry came to live at Mount Stewart, in winter she found it 'the dampest, darkest, saddest place I had ever stayed in.' So, she decided to do something about it. When Ulster landlords were encouraged to employ de-mobbed servicemen after the First World War she saw this as an opportunity to 'make the grounds surrounding the house not only more cheerful and liveable, but beautiful.' With the help of twenty new labourers she started work. In just six years they created Spanish and Italian gardens, a Shamrock garden, a Sunken garden and an art-deco style burial ground.

Alongside the south façade of the house she added the Dodo Terrace, a zoo of mythical creatures cast from concrete in the 1920s. These animals represent members of the Ark Club, an oasis for political and military figures of the time, including Sir Winston Churchill, who met to discuss contemporary issues during the First World War. Lady Londonderry set up this club, hosting dinner parties in London for all its members.

PREVIOUS LEFT
Entrance to the Dodo
Terrace.

PREVIOUS RIGHT
Two members of the Ark
Club.

ABOVE Reflections in
the Spanish garden.

RIGHT The house and
garden from the Spanish
garden.

FAR RIGHT The
Italian garden.

Wedged as it is between the lough and the sea, Mount Stewart has its own microclimate – when it rains in Belfast, on this side of the peninsula it may be clear and dry. But it does experience a high rainfall which, along with the peaty soil, suits the lush tender plants that grow here. In the spring, rhododendrons flourish alongside phormiums. Huge eucalyptus now obscure what must once have been an exposed view across Strangford Lough from the house. Their leaves rustle in the wind while olive trees, tree ferns, cordylines and trachycarpus create a romantic and tropical atmosphere.

It is remarkable that the present Mount Stewart gardens have only existed since the First World War. The lake, high up to the north of the house, was originally dug by the third Marquess in 1846 but Lady Londonderry added substantial planting. She was especially keen on plants from the southern hemisphere which explains the presence of so many eucalyptus. The oldest is a mammoth specimen of *E. globulus* planted on the Fountain Walk thirty years before she came to garden at Mount Stewart. It is almost 35m (120ft) tall, and fills the garden with a strong resinous scent. *Rhododendron magnificum* grows here along with others grown from seed collected on the expeditions of Frank Kingdon Ward. A

LEFT   Arches of
Cupressus leylandii
surround the Spanish
garden.

ABOVE RIGHT
Clipped bay trees line the
terrace above the Sunken
garden beside the house.
Gertrude Jekyll advised
Lady Londonderry on the
planting plan here.

BELOW RIGHT
Aerial view of the Sunken
garden with the red hand
of Ulster, planted with
begonias and the
Shamrock garden in the
background.

collection of olive trees were grown from seed brought back from the Mount of Olives in 1934.

To the south of the house, looking towards Strangford Lough, there was nothing apart from grass and natural woodland before Lady Londonderry created the Italian garden which runs the whole length of the house. This gaden started life with its immaculate parterres full of roses, but these foundered (possibly because of the soil), and have been replaced with herbaceous plants. Today each parterre is edged with either low-growing heathers, hebes, or purple berberis as Lady Londonderry abhorred box. The former Gardens Adviser to The National Trust, Graham Stuart

Thomas, devised the current planting plan. Particularly eye-catching are the petite deep purple *Iris chrysographes*, scarlet and orange flowered *Potentilla* 'William Rollison', *Geum* 'Fire Opal' and *Phygelius aequalis*, with its clusters of tubular red flowers with yellow throats. All is framed by two mature Irish yews, with a magnificent *Sophora tetraptera* on the east side, a New Zealand native with abundant golden yellow flowers in May.

A flight of steps leads down to the Spanish garden, a smaller area which gets its name from the green tiled *casita*, or summer house. This garden is framed on three sides by high arched hedges of *Cupressus leylandii*, planted by Nigel Marshall, the current head gardener, shortly after he took over in 1970. 'All the hedges were *Cupressus macrocarpa* but they do not like clipping, and as they got bigger it became clear,' he says, 'that we had to scrap and replant.' The hedge clipping in the garden takes Nigel and his team ten weeks.

In the Spanish garden a small oval pool, reflecting the roof of the pavilion, is stilled by the presence of the hedges. Its shape, with eight narrow rills leading off, is a copy of the ceiling in the Temple of the Winds, a magnificent private one-room banqueting house situated in the woods at the estate's east end, built in 1785 overlooking Strangford Lough.

The Dodo Terrace rises on the east side of the house above the Italian garden. Amid camellias and crinodendrons, with their drooping red flowers in summer, are the clipped and

LEFT   The spectacular
doorway to the Dodo
Terrace with concrete
figures made in the
1920s by local craftsmen.

RIGHT   The peaceful
figure of a cat beneath a
clipped bay tree on the
terrace of the house.

concrete creatures of the Ark Club. Cats cradling birds and animals of all shapes and sizes scurry around, a witty, playful layer in what is essentially a formal garden.

Tucked away behind the Dodo Terrace is the Mairi garden named after Lady Londonderry's youngest daughter, Lady Mairi Bury, who lives at Mount Stewart. This is a blue and white garden, simple and open around a central circular border, filled in spring with bluebells and primulas. The words of the nursery rhyme 'Mairi, Mairi, quite contrary, how does your garden grow?' are mosaiced around a pool in the middle. Lady Mairi was brought here as an infant in her pram and this garden feels calm and innocent, quietly planted with irises, geraniums, aquilegias, carnations and cistus.

The wild and informal Lily Wood beyond makes a wonderful contrast. The Christmas Eve gale of 1997 greatly changed this area which is rich in meconopsis, primulas, orchids and cardiocrinums. It brought down several trees including healthy elms and a young *Nothofagus antarctica,* a truly elegant ornamental tree from Chile with heart-shaped glossy leaves, was badly damaged. But the gaps have made space for new plantings of *Cornus capitata* with rhododendrons and camellias, especially *C. x williamsii* hybrids which are exquisitely beautiful and free flowering from November through to May. Eleven species of eucalyptus are planted here, and many interesting grasses including a tall bronze, clump-forming arundinaria, a wide range of ferns and several canteens full of 'General Galtieri's spinach' *Senecio smithii,* a bushy perennial with white daisylike flowers.

To the west of the house is the Sunken garden based on a design by Gertrude Jekyll who sent her designs (accepted) and planting plans (rejected) to Mount Stewart in 1921. Square and symmetrical, the area is surrounded on three sides by a stone pergola covered by an assortment of climbers such as *Actinidia chinensis, Rosa* 'Lady Hillingdon' and climbing blueberry *Billardiera longiflora.* The four beds in the centre are blue, yellow and orange and include delphiniums, lupins, tradescantias, lilies, aquilegias and geraniums, underplanted with spring bulbs. The centre of each bed holds a 3m

(15ft) Norway maple *Acer platanoides* 'Crimson King'. In early summer the whole area smells of lemon from *Paeonia x lemoinei* 'Souvenir de Maxime Cornu', a splendid yellow tree peony with a red centre. Huge tree heathers then guide you up four sets of stairs to an area ringed by vibrant orange 'Coccineum speciosum' azaleas, a formidable sight that whets the appetite for the stunning view beyond.

The clover-leaf shape of the high yew hedges of the adjoining Shamrock garden surrounds two contrasting symbols, a free-standing Irish Harp topiarised in yew, and the Red or Bloody Hand of Ulster lying flat on the gravel depicted by red fibrous-rooted begonias. The red hand is supposed to

have been that of a Scottish McDonnell who, when granted the lands of Ulster but finding himself losing a race, cut off his hand and hurled it to the Antrim shore. Adding to the drama there is an entire family hunting party cut out of the top of the yew! It is easy to see why Nigel declares 'I would not want to garden anywhere else'.

Lord and Lady Londonderry are buried in the art-deco-style burial ground, called *Tir na nóg* (The land of the ever young), above the lake. From here they can survey their garden, one of the greatest in the whole of Ireland and likely to remain so under the careful guardianship of the National Trust.

LEFT A swan floats on the lake which was dug originally by the third Marquess in 1846.

ABOVE Looking across the lake in spring, with the family burial ground, *Tir na nóg*, on the far shore.

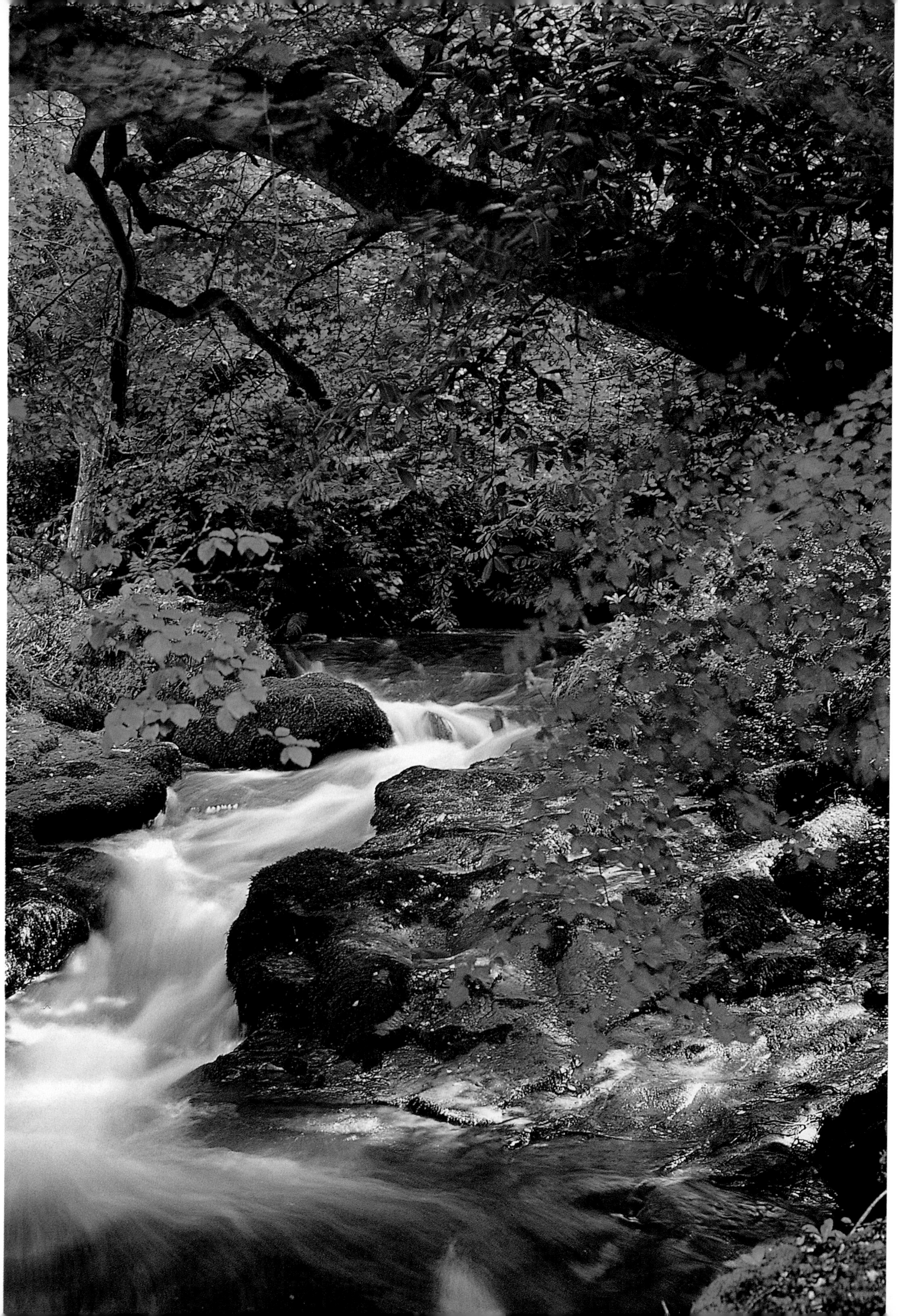

Nicholas & Susan Mosse
KILFANE GLEN

FEW GARDENERS CAN HONESTLY ADMIT TO BEING THANKFUL FOR A HURRICANE but Susan and Nicholas Mosse can. Hurricane 'Charlie' in 1986 was the big one that brought the rain that unblocked the canal that fed the waterfall that poured over the cliff and flowed past the cottage *orné* at Kilfane Glen and Waterfall garden. 'It was a very exciting moment,' explains Susan, 'all that water showed us what it looked like for the first time.' Today the waterfall crashes 10m (30ft) down to a pool, and then drains into a tributary of the River Nore which runs through the glen past the beautifully restored rustic cottage. This waterfall once formed the centrepiece of a fashionable, romantic woodland walk. Created as a 'natural' landscape, in popular eighteenth-century style, its viewpoints were carefully engineered at various points to excite the senses, inspiring wonder, mystery and fear.

The famous potter Nicholas Mosse and his wife Susan moved to Kilfane, near Thomastown in Co. Kilkenny, in 1985. From their house at the top of the glen, paths wind through dense woodland of beech and Scots pine, down steep inclines into the natural ravine. Across a small bridge over a stream, the path emerges in a hidden glade where a cottage *orné* nestles alongside the waterfall and a hermit's grotto. Guests in the heyday of the gardens in the early nineteenth century would have taken tea in the cottage before returning to the house by an alternative route.

The 8 hectare (20 acre) grounds were originally laid out by Sir Richard Power, but when the Mosses arrived the waterfall had been silent for thirty years. Susan says 'When we saw the glen we were smitten; shot through. It was pouring with rain and we could hear water and just about see the stream. But we did not actually know what we had here, a romantic valley garden. Nick loves history, so we began investigating and got bitten by the bug and restored it. When we were awarded an EEC garden conservation grant in 1993 that gave us an amazing push and our work really took off. We knew it would succeed, and visitors would want to come.'

The Mosses unearthed a series of sketches by the artist GB Miller, showing Kilfane Glen and Waterfall at its peak in 1804. These drawings provided clear designs for the cottage *orné*, and once they had unearthed its remains work began to make a perfect replica of the original. The grotto, however,

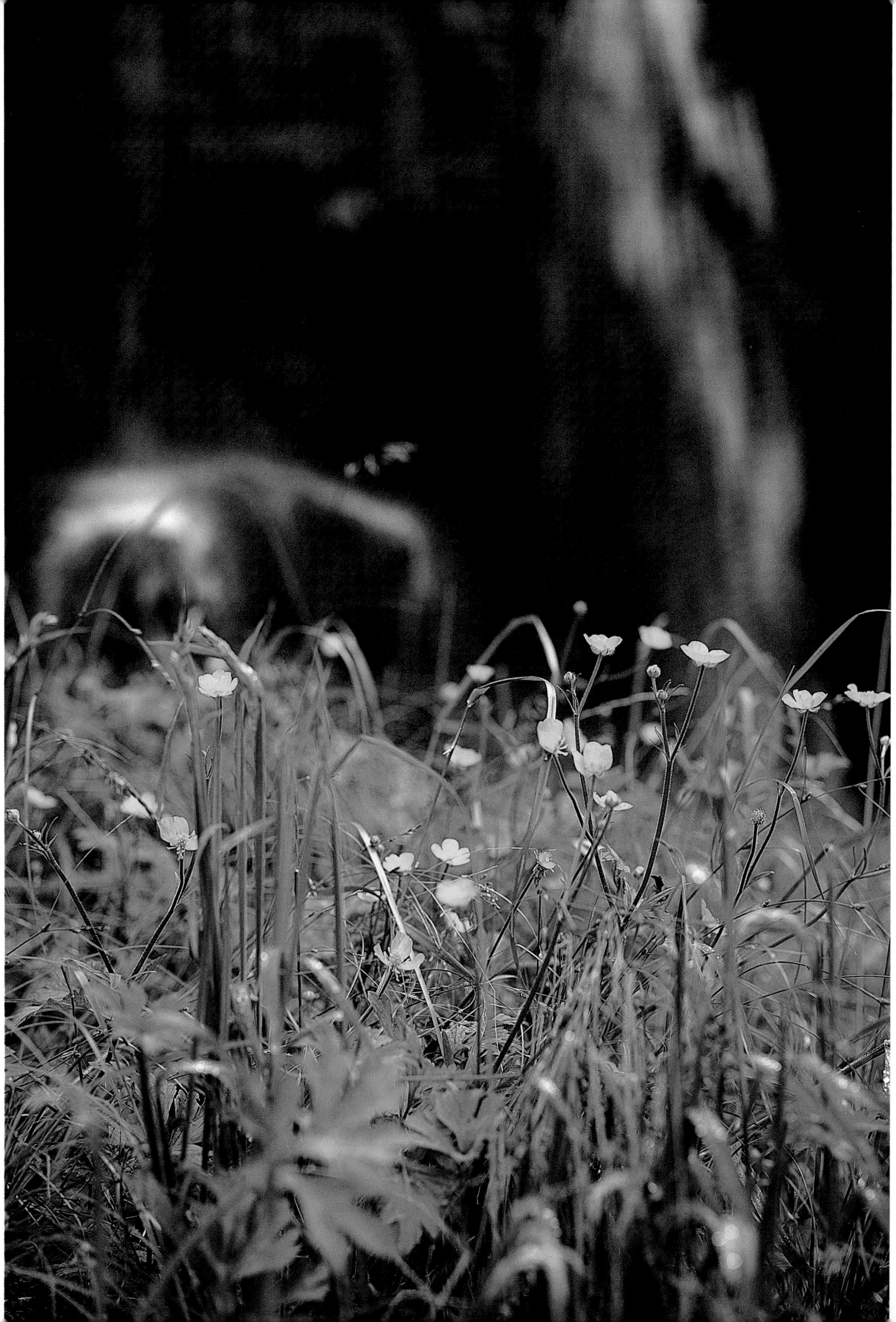

has no drawing to follow and therefore its restoration and design is still the subject of debate.

When work began the glen was in a vastly overgrown, tangled state, with one precipitous route down to the stream. Many self-sown trees were removed to make way for new paths and the small bridge over the stream that had to be crossed to get to the cottage *orné*. To feed the waterfall the Mosses had to clean out a canal 1.6km (1 mile) long. 'It was such a revelation,' Susan says, 'when the whole original design suddenly revealed itself. It was a foul winter's day and there it was, with the waterfall all going, after four years' work. I remember as we were clearing, I was both laughing and crying. I was amazed at what a good job they did then.'

The cottage *orné* is an eighteenth century concept when follies were springing up all over Europe. This particular building may well have been a place where people might have played at being peasants, influenced by the habits of

FAR LEFT Buttercups growing on the banks below the waterfall.

ABOVE LEFT The 'portals' were rescued from a compost heap and now mark the entrance to the wood from the orchard.

ABOVE ' Mr Butler's bridge'. Named after the Duke of Ormond's family who came to play here, and the Mosses' gardener Pat Butler who helped to construct the bridge 200 years later in the mid 1990s.

decadent aristocrats of France before the revolution where the Power family regularly travelled.

The restored cottage is beautifully thatched with Norfolk reeds. Period roses such as 'Old Blush China' and 'Noisette' grow over and round it, and the sound of the waterfall creates an overwhelming feeling of being part of the landscape. Sensitive new plantings of ferns are the only additions to the existing trees that include a huge *Salix alba* towering majestically over the cottage, reaching higher than the waterfall. Ash trees and birches grow out from the cliffs next to the waterfall at impossible angles, tenaciously holding on by a few roots.

The historic garden is only a part of the attraction at Kilfane. The upper garden, high above the glen, has a newer, expansive atmosphere. Even if the glen had remained undiscovered the garden would still be important. It has three different levels separated by laurel and beech hedges.

Susan Mosse describes herself as 'an art lover and an artist manqué'. She has installed some powerful pieces of art in the upper garden. A 1996 piece by David Nash called *Descending Vessel, Kilfane*, is carved out of an oak tree in the woodland behind the house in a small depression known as the cock pit. It looks as if a great bolt of lightning had opened up the tree. In the same woods is a piece by the British sculptor, Bill Woodrow, called *Rut*, along with artefacts from an earlier era including cairns, urns and little piles of stones around trees.

One fascinating piece of art at Kilfane is *Air Mass*, the work of American artist James Turrell, installed at the back of the house in 1994. It is a giant box with bench seating around the inside walls, and hidden lights in the top of the benching. It was shown in the Hayward Gallery in London and brought to Kilkenny where Turrell had a show in the public art gallery. Susan, who served on the local museum board, says, 'it was inspired by the Quaker meeting house where people would go and think. As the sky gets darker and darker it becomes bathed in incandescent light. Eventually the light starts to droop into the room like a big velvet blob.'

PREVIOUS LEFT
William Pye's water
sculpture, *Vessel III*,
came from Goodwood
sculpture park. An
inverted fountain, water
goes down into a central
funnel and then pushes
up on the outer ring to
form a flat still surface.

PREVIOUS RIGHT
A view through a
Regency-style metal
bench made by
Edward Bisgood.

LEFT   *Descending
Vessel, Kilfane* by David
Nash, who took three
days with his chain saw
sculpting out the ash tree
and then blackened it
with a propane torch to
stop it from rotting. The
sculpture will change as
the tree is still alive below
and will regrow.

Moving out of the woodland you pass through two stone portals by Sue Finlay and down three steps into the orchard, a double circle of crab apples with *Malus coronaria* 'Charlottae' on the outside, and the excellent pollinator *M.* 'Golden Hornet', which holds its fruit for such a long time, on the inside. Each tree has rings of blue muscari planted beneath it.

After the apple circles, a *Vitis coignetiae*-clad arch leads to a huge stone bird of peace nestling in the laurel hedge at the bottom of the pond garden, reclaimed by Nicholas from a salvage yard in Belfast. The pond is rectangular in shape, simple and minimalist like much else in the top garden, set off by water lilies. It leads down to the moon garden named not for its shape but because of its chiaroscuro effects of light and dark. There are mainly white flowers and plenty of dark foliage. It is designed as an evening garden because, as Susan says, 'white does funny things at night but the conditions have to be perfect.' This is where you will find most of the herbaceous plants including eucomis, known as the pineapple lily for its succulent green spikes of flowers, which Susan describes as a 'really nifty little plant', and plenty of white foxgloves, geraniums, verbascum, agapanthus, libertia, a tall, stately *Magnolia loebneri*, and a variegated pittosporum.

The lowest level of the new top garden is best known for the *Faerie's Gate*, a double-sided, perspex, mirrored piece which attracts much interest. It is approached down a long narrow alley and holds the attention as the approaching figure is constantly changing. Only for the brave!

This is an inventive garden mixing several different traditions. There are secret and artistic elements, nostalgia and history, with a clear vision for the future. Kilfane is a garden to experience and revisit. It has a strong personality and is non-competitive. In the busy and demanding world of modern horticulture, that is an unusual and refreshing quality.

David Stewart-Moore

BALLYHIVISTOCK HOUSE

IN THE FAR NORTHERN REACHES OF CO. ANTRIM, CLOSE TO BUSHMILLS and in the shadow of the Giant's Causeway, lies one of Northern Ireland's best kept secrets, the garden at Ballyhivistock House. It is the result of nearly fifty years' work by its owner, David Stewart-Moore. When he moved here with his wife in 1954 there was only a walled kitchen garden and a lawn in front of the house surrounded by a sweep of copper beeches and limes planted when the house was built in 1826.

David's first move was to dig the pond, beginning the development of what has become one of the finest examples of its type anywhere in Ireland. He used a swing shovel, which is little more than a bucket attached to a pole attached to the back of a tractor. 'It took two weeks and created an awful muddy mess, but there was a burn running through that part of the garden so I knew it would fairly soon fill up and I could get under way with planting.'

The whole garden covers 1.2 hectares (3 acres) and the pond takes up 100x20m (330x66ft), sheltered on all sides by alder, beech, rowan, ash, holm oak and pine. Few ripples trouble the water's surface bringing a serenity and calm to the scene. The mass plantings of orange, yellow and pink primulas, yellow irises and blue and pink meconopsis are completely arresting. The soil is moist and fertile yet it seems there must be some other magical element helping create such a painterly arcadia. I couldn't discover what David's secret was. When I asked him he just laughed!

The yellow flag iris *I. pseudacorus* and its variegated form spring out of the water and creep up the bank, entirely at home. The rather more delicate rich deep purple flowered *I. chrysographes* 'Margot Holmes' thrives and freely ultiplies here. Candelabra primulas abound, particularly the brilliant orange *Primula* 'Inverewe' and the yellow *P. helodoxa* and *P. japonica*, crowding right down to the water's

FAR LEFT Towers of *Gunnera manicata* grow to vast proportions in the moisture of the lakeside.

LEFT A greenhouse in the walled garden surrounded by vegetables and flowers destined for the house.

ABOVE A view across the lake with its clear reflection of the surrounding trees and flowers.

LEFT A view from the bottom end of the lake, looking towards the Monet-inspired bridge. Huge clumps of bamboo grow either side of the bridge, creating dark and mysterious tunnels to different areas of the garden. Ferns, iris leaves, skunk cabbages and gunnera burst over the bank's edge.

RIGHT Bright colours around the lake, such as these primulas, are like thick slashes of paint on an abstract painting. The flags on the left are the variegated form of *Iris pseudacorus*, their foliage reverts to green after flowering.

edge. All grow well here undisturbed. The hand of man is scarcely evident. Most exciting is the extensive collection of meconopsis on view at occasional Red Cross open days at the end of May. Self-seeding along the top of the lake are vast, arresting swathes of the yellow and red *M. paniculata*, and the intensely blue *M. betonicifolia*, some double-flowered, stunning against the more subtle pinks and pale blues of *M. napaulensis*.

David lifts and rearranges seedlings in the spring, and divides the primulas, but this is almost all the work he does down here. Helper Michelle Hall from New Zealand says 'I love the place and the plants, there is so much here that you would never see back home. The garden has a good atmosphere and that is something you can never give to a place.'

The striking bark of a clump of four Japanese white birches *Betula platyphylla* var. *japonica* sings out against the shady bank of the lake where vigorous *Magnolia campbellii* subsp. *mollicomata* seedlings peer through the taller canopy trees which shelter them from the frosts.

A simple wooden bridge supported by four telegraph poles, reminiscent of Giverny, leads into a different part of the pond garden. Shady and damp with only filtered sunlight, crowds of bobbing heads of hellebores and trilliums appear here with massive clumps of *Dactylorhiza elata* and *D.*

LEFT   One of the most
delicate and exquisite
flowers in David's garden
is the Nomocharis lily.
Its open shaped, pinkish
white spotted flowers
hang down. They thrive
in partial shade in
Ballyhivistock's rich,
well-drained soil.

RIGHT   David has
an unwitting eye for
current fashion, shown
here by his use of clumps
of grasses interspersed
with bamboo and
gunnera around the lake.

FAR RIGHT A view
through the walled
kitchen garden where
vegetables grow
alongside flowers such
as Oriental poppies
and peonies.

maderensis covering the ground in early spring. There can be few better patches of orchids in the country, their dark purple heads and spotted tongues blending beautifully with the masses of nomochoris lilies that open their blooms in tandem in summer. Eye-catching clusters of the pink flowered fern *Darmera peltata* spread along the ground, the soft light is speared by architectural yellow spires of *Ligularia tangutica* 'The Rocket', and rose-pink trusses of *Rhododendron yakushimanum* glow softly in spring and early summer. This grove also contains a *Cornus kousa* and a *Magnolia wilsonii*, the parent plant of a large collection dotted around the garden. In spring the large white bracts of the dove or pocket handkerchief tree *Davidia involucrata* flap in the wind.

The entrance to the walled garden is overseen by two more *Magnolia wilsonii*. The small flowers can be hard to see from afar, but just stand under and look up into the trees and you will spot the pure white cups and admire the rich red stamens. This section is primarily a productive area with plenty of asparagus, artichokes, beans, tomatoes, early potatoes and herbs, but ornamental plants are still given space. Two *Rhododendron thomsonii* and a *Eucryphia* x *nymansensis* mingle with azaleas and herbaceous plants.

Hidden away in a corner is a small but well-equipped propagation house where sought-after camellias such as *Camellia japonica* 'Grand Prix' and *C.* 'Nuccio's Gem' are carefully nurtured. And if all this were not enough, David, a sprightly octogenarian, has recently embarked on a new area behind the house, converting a tumbledown cattle shed into an open air garden on one side with camellias and central beds of pansies, and a covered section alongside where greenhouse plants such as abutilons are scaling enormous heights.

Ballyhivstock is a garden created with enormous energy and great expertise, with clever planting and compelling design. It is rich with colour and dripping with atmosphere, and has one of the most magical water gardens I have ever seen, a lasting testament to David's foresight and sensitivity.

Joe & Fiona Breen

SPINNERS
TOWN HOUSE

SITTING IN THE TRANQUIL 0.1 HA (¼-ACRE) COURTYARD GARDEN OF SPINNERS IN BIRR, the owners,

Joe and Fiona Breen, revealed how they came to be the proprietors of a completely new style of guest

house. 'We became so fed up with trailing around the country looking for reasonably priced, com-

fortable hotels, that we decided to open one ourselves.' Their aim was to provide the type of service

that they themselves would like to find on a trip away from home. Besides large well-designed rooms

with hand-painted decorations, enormous pillows and soft cotton sheets, they decided to make a

relaxing garden for themselves and their guests.

FAR LEFT Joe and
Fiona Breen and Fudge
the cat.

RIGHT The simple
wattle-clad raised beds
filled with lavender are
inspired by medieval
garden design. The whole
garden is created to be
easy to manage for the
busy couple.

BELOW An old
cauldron is filled with
white daisies and car-
doons and surrounded by
terracotta pots. Reclaimed
bricks add to the
Mediterranean feel of the
courtyard.

Spinners Town House is just across the road from the visitor's entrance to Birr Castle. In 1996 I went to Birr on a photography commission for *House and Garden* magazine. I needed to get into the park and garden at dawn and Joe and Fiona Breen held the key, so I dropped by, the evening before, to collect it. As is so typical of the Irish welcome, they invited me to stay for dinner and it was then that I fell in love with Spinners both as a place to stay and a beautifully calm and inspiring private garden. I asked if I might return one day to photograph, and I'm thrilled I did.

Joe and Fiona were in the clothes trade for ten years before this new venture. 'We were getting older, our clients younger, and we couldn't bridge the gap', Joe recalled. When they came across the Georgian property in Castle Street, Birr, the four terraced houses that make up Spinners were derelict. Now they are joined, and an archway leads from the street into the rectangular courtyard behind them. The courtyard garden was designed by one of Ireland's leading young garden designers, Rachel Lamb. 'Rachel must take all the credit,' says Fiona. 'We told her roughly what we wanted and left the rest to her. She has done a fantastic job. In the summer the place is bursting with atmosphere'.

The façade opposite the house hides a series of store rooms on three storeys. Once they were used for housing ani-mals, and storing wool and barrels of Guinness which came all the way from Dublin by the Grand Canal.

French windows lead out on to a raised terrace where diners can sit out. This honeysuckle- and rose-clad platform is a perfect place to enjoy the delicious bistro food and breathe in the light pineapple scent of a large *Cytisus*

LEFT AND RIGHT
Designed by Rachel
Lamb, the cobbled court-
yard is a wonderful place
in which guests can relax.
The garden is themed by
grey-slver, acid green and
purple tones which are
soft on the eye and work
perfectly to complement
the tones of the terracotta
pots, bricks, cobbles and
gravel.

LEFT The balcony of
the bistro overlooking the
courtyard is heavily
clothed in sweet smelling
honeysuckle, climbing
roses, the pineapple-
scented *Cytisus battandieri*
and a golden hop
Humulus lupulus 'Aureus'.

RIGHT The entrance
to Spinners Town House
is painted a traditionally
Irish sunny blue.

battandieri trained against the wall in the corner. A golden hop *Humulus lupulus* 'Aureus' trails over the balustrade while large terracotta pots filled with statueque silver-green leafed cardoons *Cynara cardunculus*, underplanted with annuals, are placed in the corners.

'About the only stipulation we gave Rachel was that we wanted the garden to have a Mediterranean feel.' One of the ways this has been achieved is through extensive use of cobbles. They are set into brick-edged squares and circles, and almost cover the whole courtyard. Low box hedges and beds edged with hazel hurdles separate areas of tables and chairs.

The herb garden runs down the side of the *allée* used by the Breens and their guests for games of boules. Edged with rue, it contains parsley, chives, marjoram, rosemary, sage, fennel and nasturtiums for the kitchen.

The garden is divided by a path lined with six mophead ash trees. At the top of this cobbled path is a magnificent nineteenth-century iron cauldron. Now holding a huge cardoon and a mass of white chrysanthemums, it was previously used to boil enough potatoes to feed all the workers on the neighbouring peat bogs.

To the right of the path is the outdoor theatre. The performing area is half surrounded by a semi-circular bed of perennials and shrubs. This is a bed for all seasons: pulmonarias, narcissi and the splendid Chatham Island forget-me-nots *Myosotidium hortensia* light up the spring,

leading on to a summer show of bright green-leafed aquilegias, lime green euphorbias, hostas and roses, the bed edged with purple-headed heuchera and rue. A voluminous acanthus and four upright cylinder-shaped yews give the bed good structure, while the walls are clothed with *Hydrangea petiolaris* (one of the best climbers for a shady wall) and Virginia creeper *Parthenocissus quinquefolia* which provides sensational autumn colour.

The performances that take place here vary from poetry readings and storytelling to plays performed by the Birr Georgian Society. Players emerge from the gallery which adjoins the semi-circular bed, while the audience sit in the garden amidst pots of box balls and cones of sweet smelling bay *Laurus nobilis*. The atmosphere created at Spinners is one of easy-going yet sophisticated pleasure, and it is the perfect place to stay when you visit Birr Castle demesne.

Sean O'Criadain

BALLINACARRIGA

'I ALWAYS WANTED A LONG, LOW HOUSE AT THE END OF A *BOREEN* with a garden beyond it', says

Sean O'Criadain. Today if you travel down a certain *boreen*, which is Irish for a small lane, in a well-

hidden part of east Cork you will find Ballinacarriga. It is indeed a long, low whitewashed house with

all the woodwork painted in the bright scarlet livery of Cork, and around it Sean has created a

beautiful and informal garden. With its series of garden compartments encased by high beech

hedging, it may not be what you would expect to find in a cottage garden, but Sean maintains his is

'a primitive's garden.' Despite this understatement, it is alive with colour and variety.

A warm, entertaining man now in his sixties, Sean, based in New York, has been gardening here for twenty years. 'In a cottage garden you do not need a grand plan or ornaments because that just destroys the logic. You simply need good plants and water.' He has both in his 0.9 hectare (2 acre) garden, which seems much larger because it is divided into individual rooms by 4m (12ft) tall beech hedges.

Sean's plant philosophy echoes Canon Ellacombe, author of *In A Gloucestershire Garden*. 'He and his father had a garden for ninety-nine years and their view of plants was "may the best man win".' The ebullient Sean agrees with that, 'Minimum interference is best. Let things take their

FAR LEFT Beautiful arum lilies *Zantedeschia aethiopica* have established themselves in big clumps around the pond at Ballinacarriga.

ABOVE Capped with huge pebbles, the gateway leads the eye down the first garden compartment to the boundary of beech hedging beyond. Pinks, yellows, oranges, and whites jostle together in this electrifying double border.

L E F T   The rich blue late-afternoon sky provides the perfect foil for the vibrant orange red hot pokers *Kniphofia* 'Atlanta' which grow beside the pond.

R I G H T   Pin-headed flowers of *Santolina pinnata,* an evergreen, sweet-scented shrubby bush.

F A R   R I G H T   *Astilbe* 'Bressingham Beauty'.

chances. But I do get rid of stuff that doesn't work.' If a plant is miserable it 'will be out straight away.'

The attractive white house has two wings running down into the garden. Sean grows bright red pelargoniums and deep cherry hibiscus in the windows, in flower even when I visited in April. The walls are draped with honeysuckle and *Clematis* 'Perle d'Azur' and a profusely flowering *Solanum jasminoides* 'Album' clambers all over the roof. The double borders of the upper and lower gardens below the house illustrate Sean's love of colour. 'I don't do careful colour balancing', he says. Yellow ligularia, blue anchusa and red *Lychnis chalcedonica* look entirely happy together, with pink phloxes and deep orange hemerocallis vibrating off each other, balanced by old-fashioned white campanulas and deep

pink sidalceas, with alchemilla and stachys adding a softer touch, flopping over the borders' edges. Angel's fishing rods with long wand-like stems and drooping pink earring flowers wave in the wind, while vast white-flowered Californian poppies, delphiniums and alstroemerias shove each other for room. In spring trilliums and purple orchids are early arrivals with Chatham Island forget-me-nots *Myosotidium hortensia*, a plant Sean is particularly proud of.

Sean did not want a garden designer but grants that a meeting with Jim Reynolds, of Butterstream, paid great dividends. 'Jim advised me to double the width of the borders from 2.4m (8ft) to 4.8m (16 ft). I did and that made the garden. I must pay great tribute to him for that', he says.

A huge horse chestnut tree overlooks the house and upper

garden giving some shade to the candelabra primulas that grow beneath. From the first compartment the grass path leads under a beech arch into the lower garden where two brimming borders open out, another fabulous mix of colours with brilliant orange watsonias and delicate thalictrums joining *Crocosmia* 'Lucifer' and swathes of catmint.

The pond in the third room has 'seven different kinds of dragonfly in a good year'. Here clumps of plants squeeze right to the water's edge. Zantedeschias, astilbes and rodgersias wrestle with rich green New Zealand grasses that make a satisfying rustle in the breeze. An arboretum beyond includes many native Irish hazels 'to feed the dormice'.

The cycle of rooms ends with a croquet lawn with a quince tree in each corner, a nut garden which holds the sloping rectangular compost heaps so often seen in Ireland, and a fruit garden.

Sean and gardener Billy Broderick have created an unselfconscious garden bursting with exciting combinations of colour. It is just the kind of garden you might hope to come across in this out-of-the way place.

LEFT In a good year, there are seven different dragon flies around pond in the third garden room.

RIGHT Spires of *Acanthus spinosus* Bears' breeches from this border make unusual decorations if cut in full flower.

Seán Ó Gaoithín

GLENVEAGH CASTLE

THE LANDSCAPE OF DONEGAL IS HARSH AND UNCOMPROMISINGLY BEAUTIFUL. Travelling
north-west from the bustling market town of Letterkenny, the road climbs gently through tranquil
woods and small fields until, quite suddenly, it emerges on to a barren moor, high and exposed.
Heather, stone, water and peat bog cover this land and the treeless hillsides are haunted by the
lonely cry of the curlew.

Many a visitor to Glenveagh has questioned their direction at this point, but soon a reassuring
band of conifers appears in the distance, then birch and willow promise more until the castle's drive
is revealed between tall Scots pines. The road winds for 3 km (2 miles) along the shores of the
dark-watered Lough Veagh, ending at the castle which rises majestically out of the water.

PREVIOUS LEFT
A restored Victorian metal bench nestles on the shady slopes above the pleasure gardens.

PREVIOUS RIGHT
Seán Ó Gaoithín, head gardener of Glenveagh Castle gardens.

FAR LEFT Steep stone steps lead to the upper terrace overlooking the lough and distant mountains.

LEFT *Leycesteria formaosa* is known as pheasant berry because the birds love its fruit.

RIGHT A narrow, mossy path leads to the sixty-seven steps below the View garden.

When I first met Seán Ó Gaoithín, head gardener at Glenveagh Castle Gardens, he was planting woad in the kitchen garden for a friend who is a dyer. It seemed an unlikely task, but adding to the garden's collection and experimenting with unusual plants is an important part of the job. Seán, who is an exceptionally gifted gardener, has breathed new life into Glenveagh. 'Since a garden like this will be here in fifty years' time, he says, 'its future is secure. You can do things here that you might not bother with in a private set-up when the future is uncertain.'

Glenveagh gardens were created in the 1870s by wealthy American heiress Mrs Adair following the construction of the castle. After her death the castle and its 12,000 hectare (30,000 acre) estate was bought by Henry McIlhenny in 1937. Although he only spent three months of the year at Glenveagh, he invested huge sums to improve and enlarge the garden. He continued to introduce new plants until 1983 when he gave the castle and its gardens to the nation.

Despite its short open season from May to October, Glenveagh is one of the most visited gardens in Ireland, quite a feat for a garden in the furthest northwestern corner of the Republic. It is in an idyllic setting, with a vast and open landscape facing north across Lough Veagh. The Gulf Stream climate brings 200–230 cm (80-90 in) of rain annually and steady temperatures with little or no frost, and peaty acidic soil is appreciated by thriving rhododendrons and camellias.

Seán Ó Gaoithín has studied the influence of the two men who helped transform Glenveagh under McIlhenny's patronage: the landscape designer, Lanning Roper, and the great plantsman James Russell, who introduced many rare and tender plants. Seán himself is something of a plant collector, and has so far joined expeditions to Yunnan in southwest China and to the Himalayas in the search for unusual rhododendrons and other rarities.

Lanning Roper, who for many years wrote about gardening in the *Sunday Times*, talked of the peculiar quality of light at Glenveagh, 'a misty kind of light arising from the amount of moisture in the air, giving a bluish tinge'. Seán and I stopped on our tour around the garden, to agree on this, admiring the phosphorescent light. He said 'the air is so pure that all manner of lichens grow here', as he pointed to a beautiful pale green verdigris-like example growing on a glorious Japanese maple *Acer palmatum f atropurpureum* on the lawn in the pleasure grounds.

ABOVE   An antique vase in the Italian garden.

RIGHT   The formal walled garden provides a striking contrast to the informal planting elsewhere. Clipped box hedges lead up through the garden towards the steps up to the View garden.

FAR RIGHT   A view towards the castle from the top of the walled garden.

Glenveagh is also a garden of scents. At the bottom of the glen, enclosed within its own microclimate, the strong perfume of the pinkish apricot azalea *Rhododendron superbum*, one of Russell's introductions, fills the still air. Its fragrance mingles with that of *R. edgeworthii*, the white-bloomed parent of the powerfully scented *R.* 'Lady Alice Fitzwilliam'.

In the pleasure grounds, the shelter belt of large-leafed rhododendrons and Scots pine provides ideal conditions for growing more tender plants such as tree ferns *Dicksonia antarctica*. A large *Magnolia tripetala*, or umbrella tree, with cream, scented flowers, has grown to a vast size here, joining the showy *Rhododendron falconeri*, *R. grande*, and *R. sinogrande*. A tall *R. macabeanum* bears huge trusses of bell-shaped yellow flowers.

I love the suspense of the enclosed paths linking the garden from east to west through the Italian terrace, Belgian walk, walled garden, view garden and rose garden. The latter demonstrates Seán's belief in the importance of native species and education. He has been collecting old roses from cottage gardens and says 'one day someone will walk in and identify the whole lot'. All the Donegal roses here have been propagated from what are known as 'Irish slips' – a great big

LEFT   The stone-flagged Italian terrace comes as a surprise after walking through the Himalayan Walk. Although only built in 1966, it has an air of timeless serenity with Italian sculptures bought in from Capri and large terracotta pots planted with azaleas and hostas.

RIGHT   The walled garden in the summer where lupins and sweet peas mingle with the vegetables.

FAR RIGHT   A tree fern, *Dicksonia antarctica*, in the pleasure grounds.

chunk of plant with more than a good chance of succeeding. Seán also has an old hop plant rescued from the Monastic Abbey in Donegal Town '...before the authorities put nice grass around the Abbey ruins,' he says with a wink.

The View garden looks westwards across the lough to the upper glen, an enormous saddle on the horizon which is also filled with native species. Its centrepieces are an impressive bird cherry *Prunus padus*, with small, white almond-scented flowers, and a native aspen, a tree found in old Irish woodlands which is prone to suckering. 'That is how it propagates itself,' says Seán. 'If this tree were to die another sucker up to 18m (60ft) away would be sure to take its place.'

The highlight of Glenveagh for me, is the walled garden where the woad planting was taking place. It is directly behind the castle and, unusually, faces north. Seán explains that they 'keep the soil alive by an adaptation of the lazy bed system where a 90cm (3ft) trench has manure laid on top, is single dug and mounded up. It stays like this all winter and is knocked down ready for cultivation in the spring.'

The walled garden is managed in a way that McIlhenny would approve of. 'He preserved a tradition of horticulture, and this garden is being sharply maintained in the old manner, combining fruit and flowers in the potager style,' says Seán. Less usual vegetables such as 'Purple Vienna' kohlrabi and the 'Walking Stick Cabbage' were being grown when I visited, along with more conventional fare.

Because there is no need to supply an enormous kitchen the garden's function is nowadays largely ornamental, with flowers in amongst the vegetables and herbaceous borders around the walls. Flowers feature heavily in the six box-framed square compartments that make up the centre of the garden. The impressive red striped *Dahlia* 'Matt Armour', named after a former head gardener, is grown in a double row right across two of the squares. The red *Chrysanthemum*

LEFT A pineapple on a giant column sits above Glenveagh gardens. It was placed there by McIlhenny as a symbol of hospitality.

ABOVE Seán allows some of leeks in the walled garden to go to seed.

RIGHT A spectacular view of the Gothic castle rising out of the brimming walled garden. Artichokes, beans and hollyhocks provide wonderful architectural forms.

'Ruby Mound' is still grown in honour of Henry McIlhenny, originally chosen by him because it exactly matched the colour of his study!

Despite the strong elements of tradition, Seán also experiments. He points to a group of native cabbages grown from seed collected from a cliff-top in Dorset. 'I can tell school-children that these are the parents of the common cabbages in the main beds'. His botanical training has taught him the value of passing on such information. 'Our Scots lovage comes from Tory Island, and is one of Donegal's native plants. I am building up the native flora at Glenveagh so that children can learn about their own environment.'

There are now 2,500 species thriving at Glenveagh Castle Gardens, many of them are rare, including 150 trees from the Conifer Conservation Programme in Edinburgh, and there are thousands of specimens grown from the seeds collected by Seán on his trip to China in 1996. 'We have sixty new species of rhododendron here now, such as *R. proteoides* and *R. roxianum*, thirty new sorbus, then roses, primroses (some of which were introduced to Glenveagh by the great plant hunters George Forrest and Frank Kingdon-Ward and then lost), hypericum, buddleia, spiraea and cornus. The aim is to grow and nurture all our rare plants, to save seed and then pass it around.'

The propagation area, hidden in the far eastern corner of the garden almost on the shore of Lough Veagh, is also where the Glenveagh staff will plant 2,000 native oaks to celebrate the millennium. No doubt the planting will be done by the six full-time gardeners whom, Seán says, 'give young energy to the place.'

He is highly realistic about the future of Glenveagh. 'I see myself as the keeper of the gardens. I have the responsibility for building up the diversity, the range of colours and scents but also for keeping a high standard of maintenance without altering the layout which is perfect, "maintain" and "improve" are my watchwords.'

In 1998, Seán took a sabbatical year to study botanic garden management at Kew, then travelled to South Africa for a Botanical Conference, to Nepal for plant collecting and finally to the West Coast of America to visit gardens. Now back at Glenveagh he is putting into practice newly gained knowledge. His ever-changing perspective and inquisitiveness, combined with great gardening skills, make him a noteworthy head gardener. A willingness to answer questions from visitors makes Glenveagh a welcoming, hospitable place and his passion for the whole environment gives an atmosphere of excitement and youthfulness, particularly refreshing in a state-owned garden.

Corona North

ALTAMONT

NOT MANY PEOPLE CAN SAY THEY HAVE SEEN A LEPRECHAUN. The late Corona North, former owner

of Altamont, saw one in her very own garden when she was a child, aged six. In August 1998, I sat

quietly with Corona looking over her tranquil lake whilst she told me her story. 'I was down in the

valley by the river, alone and there he was, a tiny person, chopping wood. It's hard to describe how

he looked but I remember so well how it felt. It was wonderful. He disappeared quite quickly, leaving

me surprised and delighted. I wasn't frightened and it never happened again.'

PREVIOUS LEFT
A winter view of the
garden from the bottom
of the lake looking up
the avenue of Irish yews
towards the house.

PREVIOUS RIGHT
The late Corona North
with Cosy and Udi (short
for Ugly Duckling).

LEFT   The front door
of the handsome
Georgian house, covered
in autumnal-leafed
climbers,was formerly
guarded by Corona's two
friendly Irish Wolfhounds,
Erin and Tara.

RIGHT   Dug by the
survivors of the tragic
potato famine in the
1850s, this beautiful lake
took over two years to
complete.

Life does changes pace when you spend time at Altamont, a 40 hectare (100 acre) estate 80 km (50 miles) southwest of Dublin in Co. Carlow. It belonged to Corona's family from the year of her birth in 1925, and after her death in February 1999 it was – as she wished – handed over to the Irish State.

I first met Corona in the autumn of 1996. Immediately I was entranced not only by the romance of the garden and estate but by Corona herself. I returned many times, falling in love with the whole place. The handsome Georgian house had been the site of much earlier dwellings and is a curious mixture of leftovers with courtyards, tunnels, old walls and the remnants of a chapel. Splendid trees and shrubs abound.

A magnificent lake to the rear of the house was dug using the abundant labour available during the potato famine in the 1850s, as were the 100 granite steps which rise up to it from the ancient valley below. Above the house are terraced lawns and a broad central walk with rose beds either side flanked by Irish yews clipped like tear drops.

Corona's father, Fielding Lecky Watson, was enchanted by the house and gardens after living there temporarily in 1923. Around the lake were many venerable trees which are still there today – a huge swamp cypress *Taxodium distichum* with its heavy drooping branches, and the rarer *Taxodium ascendens* as well as a Kilmacurragh cypress and a dawn redwood.

He bought the estate and, straight away, began reorganising the gardens, planting more trees, shrubs and hundreds of rhododendrons. Still flourishing today, are a fine lavender-blue flowered *Rhododendron augustinii* rising 10m (30ft) on the east wing of the house, and the exotically scented *Rhododendron cinnabarinum*, its flowers a terracotta orange. So besotted was her father with the rhododendron *genus* that Corona was named after a coral coloured hybrid introduced in 1840. The original plant is still in the garden. 'I was fortunate really, I could have ended up being called something awful like Bagshot Ruby'!

'Much of my father's collection is *chilensis* or *chinensis*, from plant hunting expeditions to Chile or China,' said Corona, 'and I wanted to go to those places too. After the war when I married and we hadn't a bean. I became a member of the International Dendrological Society. I got a letter from them one day saying they were doing a tour to Chile for the first time, costing six hundred pounds. The last letter in the post that day, which I didn't recognise and had left until last, had six hundred pounds in it as a legacy from a friend!' This extraordinary experience led to the first of many expeditions. 'One doesn't think much of a monkey puzzle growing in a Victorian garden but when you see them growing *en masse* all over a hill side they make quite a sight.'

The wide river Slaney runs along the foot of the precipitously steep Ice Age glen, where native oak trees, many very

old and tortuously twisted, entwine themselves around huge granite boulders in this ancient landscape. The lake high above fills with water from the surrounding bog and springs, its shores vivid with orange, yellow and pink candelabra primulas and other moisture-lovers such as *Hosta plantaginea*, with its 1.3m (4ft) pale green glossy leaves and late flowering white trumpets. Tiny delicate saxifrages thrive here and soft pink *Astilbe chinensis* 'Pumila' grow beneath the vast leaves of *Gunnera manicata* and blue hydrangeas.

There are special trees everywhere, a *Podocarpus salignus* with drooping branches and bright leaves with yellow undersides looks resplendent, and a dove tree *Davidia involucrata* planted by Corona fifty years ago has reached perfection. She was particularly fond of a *Cornus alternifolia* 'Argentea' and a favourite *Cornus kousa* var *chinensis*, now 6m (20ft) tall. 'The

layers of leaves are white and turn rose pink before setting strawberry seeds and turning an amazing autumn colour.' Corona talked with great knowledge and enormous pleasure of the plants in her garden. Of a Japanese snowbell *Styrax japonica* she said 'You have to walk under it to get the full effect of the seed pods hanging down.' She was rightly proud of her collection of thirty-six varieties of mountain ash, *Sorbus aucuparia*.

Corona died in February 1999 when most of her beloved fifty-two varieties of snowdrops were in flower. Hundreds of them adorned the local church at her funeral. Happily her tireless work is being continued, and Altamont, though quieter without her, stands as a fertile monument to her extraordinary life. She will be missed for a very long time, most of all by the garden.

FAR LEFT These delicate *Colchicum speciosum* burst straight out of moss on top of a wall in the courtyard behind the house.

LEFT This quirky seat, made from an old rowing boat, is now a private resting place beside the lake.

RIGHT Every detail takes on a magical atmosphere at Altamont; here an ivy stem winds its way decorously up a lakeside tree.

Brendan & Alison Rosse
BIRR CASTLE

THE LANDSCAPE OF BIRR CASTLE, CO. OFFALY IN THE HEART OF IRELAND, has a gentle presence

which envelops you as you enter, and stays with you while you explore its 40 hectares (100 acres).

It escorts you through parkland into woodland and riversides, on through meadows and past herba-

ceous borders on the castle's terraces until the senses have been thoroughly pleasured. To walk

around all the grounds takes about two hours. From the entrance gate a right turn takes you through

the park to the formal walled garden. Beyond are the greenhouses and, further on, the woodland

garden with waterfalls and Victorian fernery. The river walk takes you past a secret garden-island with

a bamboo tunnel, over a nineteenth-century suspension bridge and plantings of rare trees, then out

into the open with the castle before you.

The Parsons family acquired Birr Castle in 1620, but it was not until the late eighteenth century that the parkland was laid out, the lake dug and the first of the trees planted.

The park at Birr is one of the most outstanding of its type. The landscape has willingly accommodated countless introductions from early twentieth-century plant-hunting trips, sponsored by the sixth earl. Trees brought back from Asia and the Americas, such as *Carriera calycina*, *Magnolia dawsoniana*, *M. veitchii* and the coffin juniper *J. recurva* var *coxii*, have quite happily naturalised.

Since the park was laid out, the ground has never been ploughed, gathering stature as a wildflower meadow year on year. From spring until late July it is spectacular: bulbs, primroses, water bluebells and early orchids herald another year of cinquefoil, vetches, lady's smock, bugle, meadowsweet, herb Robert, and knapweed, while numerous grasses support a low haze of insects and pollen all summer.

PAGE 96 Birr Castle resplendent amid the surrounding wild-flower meadow.

PAGE 97 An *allée* of the four-sided hornbeam cloister.

ABOVE Victorian sculpture beneath a rose pergola in the formal garden.

RIGHT A double bench with intertwining 'R's, designed in the 1930s by the late Lady Anne Rosse.

FAR RIGHT The border, directly below the castle, includes *Echinops ritro*, *Buddleia* 'Black Knight', crocosmias, stachys, heleniums and *Solidago* 'Golden Rod'.

The battlements, in keeping with the castle, are built of mournful grey stone. Behind the façade, softened in early summer by the delicate creamy-white bracts of *Cornus kousa*, lies The Great Telescope, invented by the third earl in the 1840s, to enable him to see further into space than anyone had managed before.

The suspension bridge that crosses the River Camcor at the foot of the castle walls is another first of its type. It was built in 1810 and leads from the rich herbaceous borders beside the castle's moat to the river garden planted by the present earl's grandmother.

The herbaceous borders, planted by the present Lady Alison Rosse, include rich and vivid plantings of *Echinops ritro*, *Buddleia* 'Black Knight', crocosmias, stachys, heleniums and *Solidago* 'Golden Rod'.

No doubt helped by the rich alluvial soil in the Camcor valley, trees grow fantastically well thoughout the whole estate. The river winds underneath the tallest grey poplar *Populus canescens* in the British Isles, at 30m (100ft), and the river garden includes copper maples, handkerchief trees *Davidia involucrata* and magnolias of gigantic proportions. The magnolias have been cleverly planted to achieve continuous flowering through the season and include the early rose-pink *M. campbellii*, the delicately rose-streaked white

flowers of *M. dawsoniana* in the river garden, the small flowered *M. kobus*, and *M. macrophylla*, the heavily scented white magnolia flowering with its leafy growth at the beginning of summer.

The head gardener, Peter Hynes, was born on the estate in 1963 and trained at the National Botanic Gardens in Dublin. After a spell running a landscaping and nursery business he returned to Birr to become head gardener in January 1998, joining his father Martin who has worked at Birr for forty-five years as foreman-propagator.

Peter approaches his task with the enthusiasm of one who has a deep attachment to Birr. 'I'm keen to see what we can grow here that has not been tried before,' he says. 'Although we get prolonged frosts in the winter, we do get a lot of soft rain. I have started to grow tree ferns *Dicksonia antarctica* in the Victorian fernery in the woodland garden. It is well protected, humid and has a microclimate all of its own. If we can just protect them from the frost they'll have a good chance.'

A waterfall crashes through the fernery creating a fine spray mist. The damp atmosphere is increased by the spray from the tall plumes of a water spout, carefully concealed in the stream to hide its artificiality. A tall tree canopy of ash and oak gives shelter, creating just the right conditions for tree ferns – their tall, dark brown, almost primeval stems are a fitting addition to this slightly eerie garden which is a classic example of Victorian creative sensibilities.

In the restored formal gardens by the castle there are box parterres of intertwining 'R's which were planted in the 1930s to a specific design by Anne Rosse, wife of the sixth earl. This formidable gardener came from Nymans, a garden in the south of England (now in the hands of the National Trust) especially noted for its fine camellias and magnolias. Both *Camellia* 'Leonard Messel' and *Magnolia x loebneri* 'Leonard Messel' are both grown here at Birr and are well worth a visit in the spring.

Anne's marriage to the sixth earl, a noted dendrologist and plant collector, hailed a new era of horticulture. Work started on the formal gardens in 1935, the year the two were married. Over sixty years later the time was ripe for an over-haul: the box was removed and replaced with new plants but the design remained the same. The hornbeam *allées*, which

PAGES 100-1 An ancient *Quercus ilex* holm oak on the river bank is underplanted with *Iris sibirica* in spring.

LEFT The view over the terraces from the south of the castle.

RIGHT The early nineteenth-century suspension bridge (*entrance above right*) which joins the river garden to the lower terraces is thought to be the earliest of its kind in the world.

LEFT   The waterfall in the River Camcor which runs through the woodland garden.

RIGHT   The jubilant artificial water spouts in the restored fernery celebrate Victorian sensiblities.

form cloisters around the four sides of the terrace with windows cut into the hedging to allow views into the gravel pathed garden, also remain as they are. But the delphinium border at the top of the garden has been replanted with thalictrums and inulas as well as delphiniums.

The highest box hedges you are ever likely to see, possibly planted in the seventeenth-century, are to be found on the bottom terrace of the formal gardens. On the way up to the castle is a plant that is exclusive to Birr. *Fagus sylvatica* 'Birr Zebra' resembles the common beech in all ways except that the colour between the parallel ribs of the leaves is not green but yellow. This gives an unusual striped effect. A chance seedling found at Birr has given shoots which are to be grafted on to rootstocks to increase the numbers of this splendid tree.

The present earl talks with wonder of this and the other 3,000 plant species at Birr, harking from all parts of the globe, 'From the tamarisk of Alaska, through the evergreen oaks of the Arizona desert, to the nothofagus or the southern beech'. As he is an intrepid traveller and plant collector himself, we are lucky that he has the strong commitment to continue the plant-collecting traditions of his forebears.

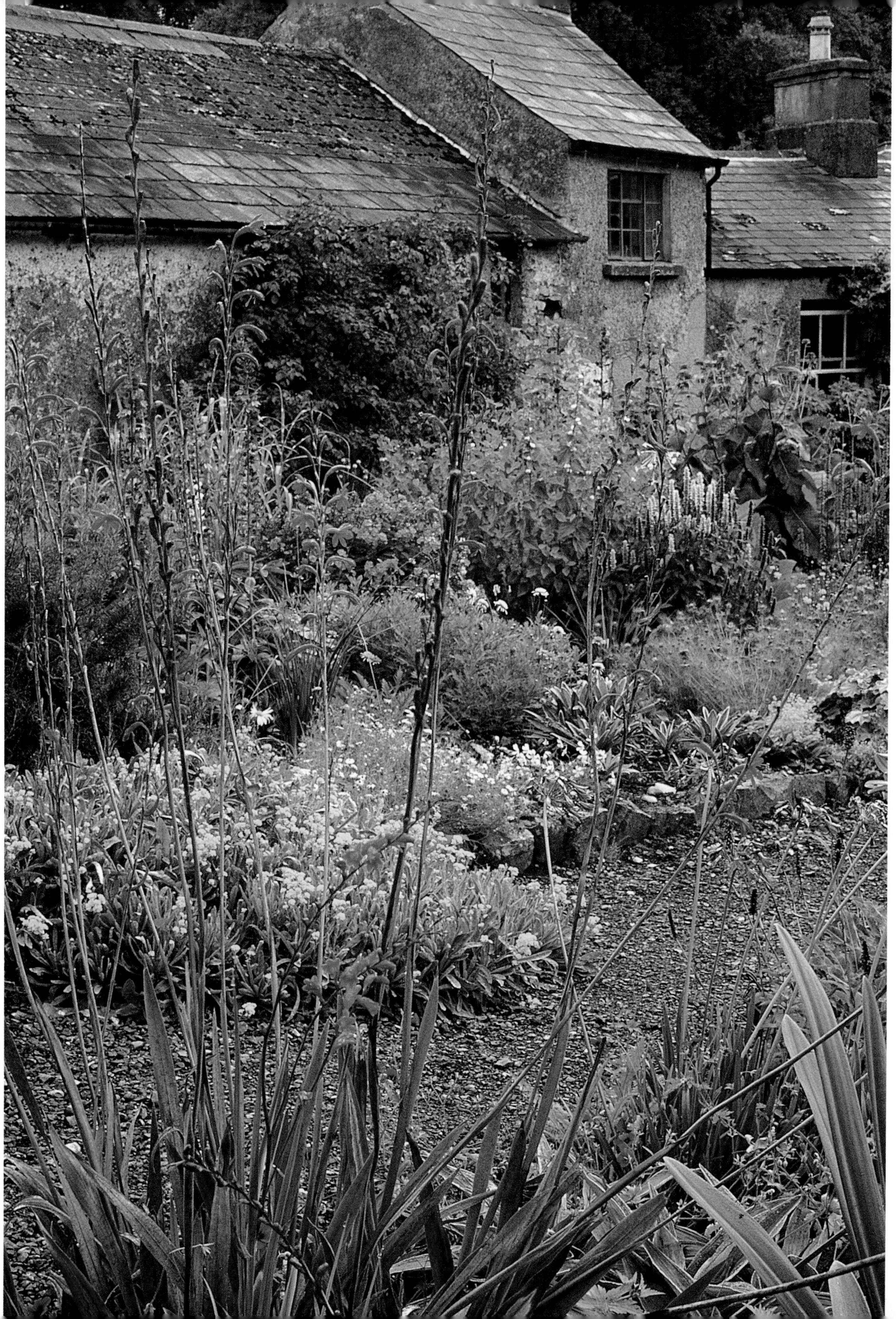

Jonathan & Daphne Shakleton

LAKEVIEW

IN AMONGST THE DRUMLIN HILLS NEAR MULLAGH IN CO. CAVAN, Daphne and Jonathan Shackleton have created a stunning garden at Lakeview that suits this strange and beautiful landscape. Their garden is carved out of one of these mysteriously shaped hills and runs down through wood and meadow to meet the shores of Mullagh Lake.

Here on stony fertile soil, the remarkable Shackletons continue the major contribution their family has made to Irish horticulture over six generations. Jonathan's father, David, was one of the outstanding plantsmen of this century. His garden at Beech Park in Clonsilla, west of Dublin, held a collection of over 4,000 species of rare and tender plants, started in the 1930s. Included were over thirty different species of celmisia, the New Zealand daisy, ranging from the large, silver-leaved *Celmisia semicordata* 'David Shackleton' to the tiny *C. sessiflora* 'Mount Potts'.

When Beech Park was sold in 1995 Jonathan, Daphne and their three children moved to the farm at Lakeview. To keep David's collection in the family, they took cuttings and root divisions from as many plants as possible, but left the majority of plants behind for the new owner of the property. Along with the Georgian house, outbuildings and barns at Lakeview, came 120 hectares (300 acres) of farmland – now divided between forestry and a herd of cattle that Daphne is rearing organically.

Once work on the house was complete and the farm up and running, Daphne began planning the new garden. The Shackletons work on different areas at Lakeview, Daphne creates the overall effect and runs a plant nursery, and Jonathan works with trees, shrubs and climbers.

To the front of the house a wildflower meadow sweeps down towards the lake, awash with soft purple crocuses in

PREVIOUS LEFT
'A jumbly mass of cottage garden favourites' in the border that runs behind the house, including pink phloxes, orange *Watsonia pillansii* and some small silver-leafed celmisias.

PREVIOUS RIGHT
Daphne surrounded by herbaceous perennials.

FAR LEFT   The path of the main double border which runs the length of the garden.

LEFT   Rebel the terrier.

RIGHT   Swordlike Iris leaves and yellow mopheaded *Tanacetum parthenium plenum* stand beside vibrant red monardas and *Verbena bonariensis* at the back of the walled garden.

the spring. To the rear, in the 0.4 hectare (1 acre) walled garden, a thick jungle had spread over the terraces which were cut into the hillside in the 1930s. Reluctantly, Jonathan and Daphne resorted to spraying this area with a systemic herbicide to enable planting to begin.

While the terraces were slowly being restored, other construction work began with the help of their farmworker, Joe. Parts of the surrounding 120cm (4ft) stone walls were rebuilt and paths and borders were created. Rather like Beech Park, Daphne has created vast sweeps of double herbaceous borders running over 30m (100ft) away from the house. With another double border crossing at an intersection one third of the way down, the basic plan of the garden is cruciform.

Returning to Lakeview at the end of August 1998, I was astounded by the garden's transformation from wilderness to paradise in scarcely three years. It is now breathtakingly beautiful. Herbaceous perennials swell the borders, perfectly balanced in colour, form and height. Huge towers of *Artemesia lactiflora* with frizzy white flowers combine well with the glaucous blue-green foliage of *Thalictrum lucidum*, another stately plant, and lime-green *Kniphofia*, an unusual variety of the red hot poker. These mingle with the soft yellow pea flowers of *Lathyrus luteus* and big helenium daisies in the yellow section of her border.

Nothing looks out of place here, the overall effect is natural and harmonious, the atmosphere serenely peaceful.

Daphne uses a perfect blend of highly knowledgeable yet instinctive planting.

Whilst cuttings were taking root and pieces of plants from Beech Park were clumping up in the field at the side of the house, Daphne started work planting the walled garden. On the side of the old yard buildings. she has created an area 6m (20ft) deep with, as she puts it, 'a jumbly mass of cottage garden favourites'. Among the mass is sweet rocket *Hesperis matronalis*, clustered with pale pink and white scented flowers in the spring followed by delphiniums, old-fashioned highly scented sweet peas, many different phloxes in shades from soft shell pink to vibrant lilac, and in late summer the imposing spires of Culver's root *Veronicastrum virginicum*.

FAR LEFT
The spectacular *Artemesia lactiflora* with frothy milk-coloured flowers stands 2m (6ft) high, thriving in Daphne's rich soil.

CENTRE Evening primroses *Oenothera stricta* 'Sulphurea', are planted at each corner of the inter-secting paths.

LEFT The delicately arching form of the grass *Molinia caerulea* subsp *arundinacea* blends with flowering perennials in the herbaceous border.

In the lower section of the cruciform shape, a beautiful mulberry tree stands beside a perennial vegetable and herb bed. Daphne has chosen a more formal theme here with neat box edging containing varieties of artichokes for their shapes and colours, asparagus, chives and alpine strawberries.

On the restored stone-faced terraces, spring planting takes precedence with a host of early hellebores and blue poppies, *Meconopsis x* 'Slieve Donard' mingle with delicate early peonies such as the lemon-coloured Caucasian peony, *Paeonia mlokosewitchii*, the shocking pink *P. arietina* and the blush pink *P. willmotiana*. Daphne also grows trilliums and ginger plants such as *Roscoea humeana* for their orchid-like blueish purple or yellow flowers.

The paved area between the terraces is bursting with small delicate flowers. Daphne and her twelve-year-old daughter Hannah added to these in the spring of 1999, hoping that the tiny violas, dianthus and numerous alpines would manage to survive dogs' paws and unsuspecting visitors.

Below the terraces at the base of the walled garden is a moist area shaded by beech trees, perfect for damp-loving plants such as the bronze-leafed rodgersia. This is Daphne's woodland garden. Its backdrop of laurel gives a strong contrast to the drifts of shade-loving perennials and ferns, with hostas, acid green and purple euphorbias, pulmonarias, with their small pink, blue or white spring flowers and spotted leaves, and the exquisite *Arisaema candidissima*.

LEFT   Deep carmine
pink *Lobelia* 'Tania'
flowers in August in the
rich moist soil of the
main herbaceous border.

RIGHT   At the top of
the garden Daphne grows
her vegetables amidst
various reminders of the
old garden that used to
belong to her aunt, such
as the old roses which
clamber over pergola.

With a polytunnel next to the stock beds, Daphne propagates plants for sale and visitors can buy delicious Oriental poppies such as *Papaver orientale* 'Curlilocks', or some of the plants that were grown at Beech Park like the large variety of Irish cultivars of phloxes. Although she has local workers helping with the potting on, the majority of the nursery work is done by Daphne. With great skill, she collects seeds, divides plants and roots cuttings, bringing in new plants from other gardens or specialist nurseries to expand her own stock. Some of her plants also go to garden restoration projects or new designs she is involved with.

Below the nursery, an old established orchard is home to her geese and Jonathan's bee hives, underplanted with a wild meadow. The whole garden feels loved and nurtured as do the children, David, Jane and Hannah, their animals and the family's herd of cattle. Daphne wakes early and throughout her working day nothing, from the seedlings in her nursey to the health of the ponies, escapes her caring eye.

Although Daphne is rather private and would prefer to garden quietly at Lakeview, her brilliant plantsmanship means that people search her out and come to buy plants and catch a glimpse of Lakeview's utterly magical garden.

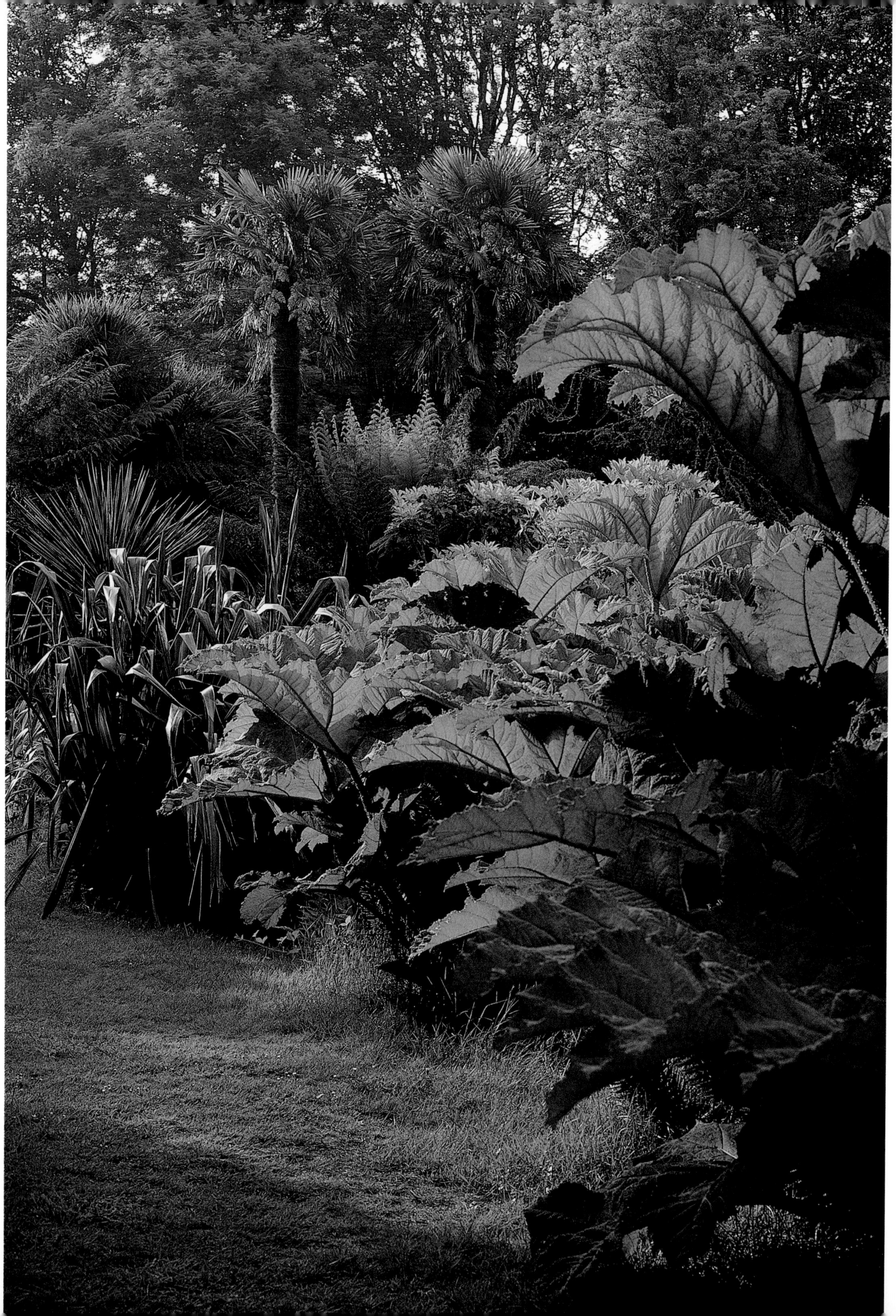

Martin Sherry
CREAGH

THE TEMPTATION TO SNEAK THROUGH A PAIR OF WROUGHT IRON GATES, past the lodge and up the drive is hard to resist in Ireland. It is nigh on impossible when beckoned on by the sight of large flame-red flowers of the Chilean fire bush trees *Embothrium coccineum* on either side of the drive. If you make a tentative move at first, stop the car and wind down the window, you become seduced by delicious scents. The smell is incredible, comforting, inspiring: it is the salt air of the sea and the old established perfume of acres and acres of damp trees. It lifts the spirit and creates the thrill of heightened expectation. There is no going back, for this is Creagh, the jewel that lies between Skibereen and Baltimore at the very tip of west Cork. It is one of the most romantic gardens in southern Ireland.

PREVIOUS LEFT
Expansive and theatrical *Gunnera manicata* forms part of the semi-tropical enclosure at the base of the garden.

PREVIOUS RIGHT
The dogs at Creagh, (*from left to right*) Henry, Frederick, Rocky and Miss May, all have their own sun-loungers in the garden, imported from Italy.

LEFT   The serpentine mill pond which winds beside the estuary is overhung by beech and weeping willow.

RIGHT   Chusan palms *Trachycarpus fortunei* and tree ferns *Dicksonia antarctica* grow tall in the warmth of the Gulf Stream garden at Creagh.

I last went to Creagh after staying in the hyper-charged atmosphere of Darina Allen's Ballymaloe Cookery School. The difference in tempo was extraordinarily marked.

As you round the final bend of the drive you catch the first of many glimpses of water. It is the estuary of the River Ilen and in it the Island of Inishbeg, a solid buffer to the south-westerlies which gather pace far out to sea where St. George's Channel meets the Atlantic.

Perhaps it was this first, tantalising view that lured the former owners, Peter and Gwendoline Harold-Barry, to purchase these gardens in 1945. It may have been the warmth of the Gulf Stream which allows exotica such as the castor oil plant *Ricinis communis* to flourish when inland they might not survive. Or maybe, the rich acid soil, perfect for growing rhododendrons such as the rare *R.* 'Kilimanjaro' which produces chocolate-red flowers from late spring to early summer? Perhaps it was the romance of the serpentine mill pond that attracted them. Whatever it was, we can only be grateful as it was this couple from Kilkenny who created the romantic structure of the present garden.

The oaks, beeches and limes were already in place when the Harold-Barrys moved in. Beneath this canopy were great

garden tells a different story. Far from the wild romance of the main plantings, this is a productive garden where convention and regimentation rule. When restoration began the paths here were intact, there was a little in the way of soft fruit and potatoes for the house, but otherwise it was wild. Now resplendent rows of organic vegetables grow in straight lines between neatly clipped box hedging, and espaliered apples and pears border the paths. The centrepiece of the kitchen garden is the palatial 'Hen Hilton'. Feathered

residents amble happily around their spacious grounds and are an attraction in themselves. It is encouraging to see this productive garden restored to its former glory rather than joining many others as a wilderness.

The majority of work at Creagh, from building glasshouses to dredging ponds, is carried out by a team of local workers on a special government-run employment scheme but there is a lot of work to do in 8 hectares (20 acres) of garden and woodland. The gale of Christmas Eve 1997 put

paid to eighty trees, serious damage for a place so exposed and potentially fragile.

There is no specific route around Creagh. Once inside the gates one feels enveloped in its free-wheeling atmosphere; follow any path and it will bring an unexpected view or plant of interest. This is not a grand formal garden that demands to be seen at a specific time of year, or looked at in a particular way. It is a calm and peaceful place – old world Ireland, untouched by modernity.

FAR LEFT   The delicate spines of a conifer.

CENTRE   A vine leaf presses against one of the green house windows, misty with condensation.

RIGHT   Flower head of *Gunnera manicata* – Chilean rhubarb.

Sarah & Robert Guinness

LODGE PARK

SOMEWHERE BEHIND THE HOUSE AT LODGE PARK, STRAFFAN, CO. KILDARE, are the remains of a formal garden created when the house was built in 1773. It is now buried under a sumptuous wild-flower meadow and is likely to remain undisturbed for a good while longer as attention is diverted to the restored walled garden. Lodge Park now belongs to Sarah and Robert Guinness, who are helped by their gardener Patrick Ardiff.

The walled garden is a 0.8 ha (2 acre) rectangle with high high mellow brick walls, reached through imposing iron gates; it has style in abundance. Even though the public are welcomed in to see it, the mood somehow feels intimate and secluded.

LEFT A close-up of the
Datura aurea 'Angel's
trumpet', that does so
well in the greenhouse at
Lodge Park.

RIGHT A lichen-
covered sculpture of
Aphrodite stands at the
end of the garden.

One gets the feeling the walled garden is Sarah Guinness' domain, while her husband's heart is with the Straffan Steam Museum which he set up in a reclaimed church in the yard at the back of the walled garden. The first thing you notice is the lean-to propagation house sitting comfortably in the 60m- (65yd-) long, south-facing shrub border. The building is immediately next to an asparagus bed, and is flanked on both sides by ancient, beautifully espaliered pear trees which grow to the top of the high walls onto which they are trained. They may no longer fruit heavily, but the gnarled old

L E F T Imposing gate-
way opening the way to
the walled garden with a
view all the way down
the main path.

A B O V E R I G H T A
bench in a quiet corner
of the garden overhung
with *Wisteria sinensis*.

R I G H T The blue and
yellow border: the flowerheads of agapanthus
about to open out and
below it the blue bell-
shaped flowers of
Platycodon grandiflora.

branches look wonderful. The propagting house is still very active. It is full of seed trays and freshly raised young plants, everything overseen from one corner by a bright orange Bird of Paradise *Strelitzia reginae* with its pointed beak and beady eye, a classic greenhouse plant.

In the centre of the walled garden is the vinery, built in 1834 and now perfectly restored. Sadly the vines no longer exist but you can still see evidence of where they grew.

In the roughly mown orchard of apples and quinces there is a metal summerhouse-type structure, covered by the apple-scented, vigorous rambler *Rosa* 'François Juranville' and *R.* 'Félicité Perpétue' with its blush-pink clusters of double rosettes. The top is adorned with an impressive wrought iron rosebud finial, designed for Sarah by her husband.

Nothing is rushed in this garden. Plants are allowed to take their time and settle in, and the results speak volumes. The kitchen garden is well established and Sarah grows seventy five per cent of all her fruit and vegetable requirements; her top choice of salad potatoes include 'Ratte' and 'Pink Fir Apple' which successfully store right through winter. The vegetable garden is partitioned into four squares by head-high espaliered apples which run along the cruciform paths. 'Lord Derby' and 'Grenadier', cookers and eaters respectively, run side by side. One square contains potatoes, the second soft fruit (raspberries, black and redcurrants, and gooseberries), the third an assortment of onions, leeks and celeriac, while in the fourth, red and green lettuces are arranged in formal lines. The espaliered apples are underplanted with herbs. In summer the grey-green foliage of sea kale *Crambe maritima*, appears alongside.

Most of the horticultural work is left to Patrick who has been with the Guinnesses for eight years since leaving the Botanical Gardens in Dublin. Relaxed and confident, he has the same outlook as his employers: 'If it does not work out this year, it will next year. We have never had an argument, but I call the border under the north wall 'Siberia' as all the orange plants have been unfairly moved there!'

There is a wide range of hot colours in the Siberian

border. The dark-stemmed, yellow-flowering *Kirengeshoma palmata* makes its presence felt. This native of Japan has a controlled, expansive shape, with spiky leaves shaded from dark green to purple at the tips, perfectly overlapping in layers on reddish-purple steams. The purple-flowered aquilegias 'Magpie' and 'William Guinness' have quite startling depth of colour, as does the fiercely coloured red dahlia 'Bishop of Llandaff' .

The white garden is Patrick's favourite area. The delicate *Geranium sanguineum* 'Album' performs well here with the more exotic celmisias from New Zealand, *Papaver orientale* 'Perry's White', *Incarvillea* 'Snowtop', *Lysimachia ephemerum* with its tall white fronds, white Jacob's Ladder *Polemonium caeruleum album* and white cistus. All are overhung by the sumptuously flowering white *Wisteria sinensis*.

Sarah herself is most proud of the south-facing border, near the 90m (98yd) gravel pathway which runs down the length of the garden, containing a mixture of shrubs, trees and herbaceous plants. The key performers are an early yellow-flowering silver mimosa *Acacia dealbata*, the pineapple-scented *Cytisus battandieri*, a hardy corokia from New Zealand, ceanothus, and several huge globe artichokes and shrub roses.

The path is lined on either side by low box hedging and yew pyramids, much taller than head height, this structural elegance creates a grand formal walk throughout the year. At the end a pair of gates echo those at the path's entrance, a tennis court appears on the far side next to a mixed herbaceous border which includes the biggest *Crambe cordifolia* plant I have ever seen. Patrick puts its size down to

the amount of rain which also encourages the phloxes – such as the variegated 'Norah Leigh' – to do well and so too the robust clumps of *Agastache mexicana* with their purple fuzzy heads, and Penstemon 'Alice Hindley'. The huge thistle-like onopordums and eryngiums indicate an eye for the current fashion for architectural plants.

Visitors walking along the path underneath the north wall will find a marvellous yellow, white and blue border awash with delphiniums and cephalaria including the large yellow *Cephalaria gigantea*. Plants arrive from good nurseries in Ireland and England, or as gifts from friends – the odd-shaped sorrel found here came from Darina Allen and the pericallis in the vinery is from Helen Dillon.

This border is new and contains some good plantings of verbascum, *Helictotrichon sempervirens* and other blue grasses and hostas such as the strong dark blue *H.* 'Krossa Regal'. *Corydalis cheilanthifolia*, *Meconopsis betonicifolia* and *Papaver orientale* 'Karine' which have begun to bulk up and give the border some shape. A dark red rose 'Souvenir du Doctor Jamin' likes the shade under the north wall.

The garden design is still ongoing. Down by the entrance to the museum Patrick hopes to remove the limy soil, replace it with acid soil and introduce spring-flowering shrubs, such as camellias and azaleas, that only thrive in these conditions.

The willingness to experiment, and the constant search for new, interesting plants are what make the garden such a beautiful place. Add to this a high standard of maintenance, four protective walls, a keen eye for design and a great deal of pleasure taken in carrying out the work, and you realise what makes this such an exceptional garden.

Darina & Timmy Allen
BALLYMALOE
COOKERY SCHOOL

DARINA ALLEN'S BALLYMALOE COOKERY SCHOOL AT KINOITH in Co. Cork is more than simply an internationally renowned cookery school, a splendidly diverse garden, and a staggering success story. It is a phenomenon. What began as a few cookery lessons in the stable yard of an attractive Regency house has become one of Ireland's most successful businesses.

Ballymaloe lies between Ballycotton and Shanagarry, a twenty-five minute walk from the east Cork coast. The climate is mild, the rainfall high and the soil neutral. It makes good growing country, and the first thing you learn from Darina is that 'good food can only come from the highest quality and freshest ingredients possible.' What better place than her own garden?

TOP LEFT Lovage
shoots in the herb garden.

LEFT   Darina's son Isaac
made this metal tepee.

RIGHT   The extensive
formal herb garden in
early autumn.

The enthusiasm of Darina and her staff is infectious. Her eyes sparkle behind neat designer spectacles, and her quicksilver brain is capable of processing fantastic amounts of information. The moment you enter the grounds at Ballymaloe you are gripped by the charge that fuels the place. Bustle and noise from humans and animals continues right through the day.

The first person you will probably see is Eileen O'Donovan cutting herbs at eight o'clock in the morning, except everything is blurred as she whizzes past at top speed on her way to the kitchens. Or it may be Darina's husband Timmy, baking bread at dawn. No time to stop, there are animals to feed, cows to milk, vegetables to pick, lessons to give and long herbaceous borders to weed! Teamwork and spirit is what Ballymaloe thrives on.

Darina and Timmy married in 1970 and moved to Kinoith. There was already an interesting garden there as Timmy's father had planted a substantial commercial apple orchard of interesting varieties, and erected several acres of mushroom houses and timber-framed glasshouses for tomatoes and cucumbers. In the early 1980s, Timmy started a farm shop and pick-your-own site offering apples, raspberries, blackcurrants and gooseberries. Meanwhile Darina started giving cookery classes in the outbuildings.

As profits grew, the couple started to restore and improve what had once been a fine, early nineteenth-century garden. They began with the original pleasure garden. It contained a nut walk, (sadly, only one walnut survives), a summer house with a stunning mosaic floor, and a pond. But the undergrowth was so dense it was six years before these

treasures were unearthed! The hedges were eventually tamed with chainsaws and clipped to give a sense of order whilst the garden inside remained wild and overgrown. From the adjoining herb garden you will now see spring blossom and a tunnel of fragrant cherries leading to a white seat beside the pond 70m (225ft) away.

Among the pleasure garden's many interesting older trees and shrubs is a fine specimen of the Chilean lantern tree, *Crinodendron hookerianum*, the expansive and prostrate *Viburnum plicatum* f. *tomentosum*, and splendid cherries including the Japanese *Prunus* 'Shirotae', a beautiful, fragrant double white. *Magnolia wilsonii* and the snake-bark maple

Acer pennsylvanicum have been more recently planted. A swathe of blue Russian comfrey *Symphytum* x *uplandicum* grows beside the pond at the end of the garden, behind which towers a gigantic tulip tree *Liriodendron tulipifera*, a folly tucked under it. And then the herb garden hits you.

By the mid-1980s work had started here. It took two years to clear and clean the site, and prepare the soil for planting. The design was based on famous chef Robert Carrier's own herb garden, and Villandry in France. The huge Ballymaloe garden took shape from sketches on the back of a cigarette packet! It took 10,000 box plants to make the forty box-edged compartments which hold a staggering array of herbs,

FAR LEFT 'Puppy'
peruses for mice in the
clipped bay and
nasturtiums flowers
of the potager.

LEFT A hen and her
chicks scratch freely in
the herb garden.

ABOVE A surprise
discovery of a nest of eggs
in a pot of rosemary out-
side the cookery school.

all of which are used in the school and Garden Café. As well as the obvious, they grow rue, anise, caraway, cumin, hyssop, angelica, chervil, good King Henry, sweet cicely, summer and winter savory, and wormwood. Both the herb and the pleasure gardens can be viewed from the rustic tree house.

The potager is almost a secret garden, hidden behind a screen of trees half-way up the drive between the house and the cookery school. Diamond shaped, it is dissected by herringboned brick paths, the beds filled with ornamental and edible flowers including geraniums and nasturtiums, and salad vegetables. The increasing demand for oriental vegetables is marked by the presence of pak choi, mizuna and Californian mustard greens. Winter colour and structure is provided by globe, Chinese and Jerusalem artichokes, purple Brussels sprouts, purple and white sprouting broccoli, and sea kale crowns under their terracotta forcing pots. All areas of the garden are being converted to organic production.

The fruit area was designed by Darina's friend Jim Reynolds as a garden for all seasons. It is underplanted with spring bulbs including *Iris reticulata*, scillas and snowdrops, and violets which were once grown as a commercial crop, now crystallized for the kitchen. Metal arches support espaliered 'Irish Peach', 'Lane's Prince Albert', 'Arthur Turner' and 'Egremont Russett' apples. Peaches and apricots grow against the wall. There are black, white and redcurrants, boysen and tayberries, yellow and red raspberries, alpine and dessert strawberries, plums, medlars, quinces, figs, pears, damsons and 'Nashi fruit', a cross between an apple and pear.

The vast 0.4 hectare (1 acre) glasshouse is the engine room of the edible garden. Here potatoes and parsley, salads and spinach, broccoli and beans, tomatoes and turnips, carrots and cucumbers grow year-round for the cookery school and café. Susan Turner the new head gardener, formerly of Ryton Organic Gardens in England, keeps the area pest- and disease-free with biological controls.

A huge 45m (150ft) herbaceous bed in front of the house-leads to the shell house. 'I developed my passion for collecting shells from being so far from the sea as a child,' says Darina. This tall octagonal building was designed by Darina with shells set in place by Blot Kerr-Wilson. But perhaps the grandest idea of all at Ballymaloe is the developing Celtic maze given by Darina to Timmy as a birthday present. 'Timmy was not impressed because he knew he would have to pay for it!' When this beautiful and inch-perfect creation of Irish yew *Taxus baccata* 'Fastigiata' grows up, and the herbaceous plants swell and flower, they will make perfect subjects to the regal shell house watching over them as the days at Ballymaloe race past at a furious pace.

The whole place glows with vibrancy and fresh energy. Achieved through determination and passion, Ballymaloe Cookery School is a unique experience which inspires foodies and gardeners alike.

LEFT A view across the potager, with beds laid out in squares and diamonds, edged with bricks.

RIGHT The majestic beech hedges and door-ways are seen here from 'Lydia's garden' looking into the herb garden.

Helen Dillon

45 SANDFORD ROAD

MOUNTING THE STEPS OF 45 SANDFORD ROAD for the first time is a daunting but exhilarating exercise. Behind the door is Helen Dillon. Not just a big player in the game of Irish horticulture, she is a genuine high roller. Broadcaster, TV personality, writer, lecturer, designer and plant hunter, Helen is formidably expert at everything she does. Her Dublin garden is an immaculate example of the possibilities of gardening on the east coast of Ireland. The first time I came through the door I was carrying the cumbersome metal step-ladder I use for photography. It was 1995 and I was travelling around Ireland on a Merlin Trust scholarship photographing gardens. Wandering around the garden with my sister and a gardening friend Neil, we were mortified when Helen came flying out of the house berating us for knocking her plants with the ladder. Luckily since then our relationship has been on a firmer footing and Helen is one of the most entertaining and informative of gardening friends.

Helen's nature is inquisitive, 'What's another word for com-binations?' she asked, blowing clouds of smoke from her umpteenth cigarette of the day. 'I loathe that phrase "plant combinations'". Before I could respond, she had warmed to her task and asked what I thought of phormiums. 'Well, you do see them more and more on roundabouts...' I offered tentatively. 'You're right' she said, as if I'd passed a test. Then the conversation really began. 'If someone gave me ten acres, I would be growing fields of hellebores and no-one would hear of me again.' Hardly. This self-effacing banter is typical; Helen is rather shy, though incredibly charming and funny.

Every inch of the garden has been meticulously planned and designed, form and colour are vital, and she is not afraid to make changes. 'I wait until something annoys me, and then I tear it to bits and start again. I fear the garden becom-ing static, if it does you merely become a curator; you have to keep trying new ideas.' Helen's style of gardening is very precise. She has been gardening here for 25 years and in that time has nurtured various microclimates including raised alpine beds and areas where acid-loving plants flourish.

Her appreciation of the tried-and-tested does not dampen her ardour for rare and interesting plants. *Tropaeolum poly-phyllum* runs over one of her raised beds, copying an effect she first saw in Chile. Nearby is a delicate, glaucous leafed member of the sea kale family, *Crambe filifolia,* brought back from Seattle. Next to that is a variegated lily-of-the-valley *Convallaria majalis* found in Cornwall, which took 'a long time to get going', and a perennial kale given to her by Darina Allen from the Ballymaloe Cookery School gardens.

Helen strongly believes in protecting the welfare of plants that might be endangered or in decline; the silver-leafed New Zealand daisy *Celmisia semicordata* 'David Shackleton', is one case in point. She tends a plant carefully until it has given lots of cuttings, after that she feels she need not grow it any more if she doesn't want to. She also propagates for security in case she loses the plant. It is possible to buy several endangered plants from her yard and a trip to Sandford Road is often fruitful for the gardener with an eye for a rarity such

as the showy *Arum creticum*. You can always find good helle-bores in the spring.

There are few spaces in this intricately designed, cleverly planted area, approached via a long lawn, tended beautifully by her husband Val. At the top end is a gently bubbling cir-cular pool with a mere handful of pebbles under the shallow water. Built after a trip to Morocco, its simple Islamic form brings a sense of peace to the heart of this city garden. Beyond is a tunnel of roses, honeysuckle and apples. The lawn is flanked by mixed borders, one red, one blue – both spectacular.

In the red border the superb semi-double bright red dahlia 'Bishop of Llandaff' joins bronze leafed, red stemmed *Rodgersia pinnata* 'Superba', pin-cushion headed scabious 'Chile Black' and ginger lilies *Hedychium coccineum*. This bor-der reflects a powerful creative side of Helen's personality – a riot of fiery colour. Opposite, cool shades of conventional blue delphiniums, campanulas and salvias reveal a more rational and formal side.

Plants are carefully chosen because of the limited space, and they all receive star treatment. Few die, but if they have got to go then they must die 'gracefully', as Helen puts it.

Gladiolus byzantinus however dies 'very badly' and 'you have got to be very careful where you put colchicums.' All this knowledge comes from years of experience. 'Twenty-five years,' she adds, 'is an awfully long time in gardening. The longer you tend the same garden, the better you have got to become. To begin with it is dead easy – fresh soil, things grow, wonderful. Then suddenly it gets too crowded and that is when you have got to learn to think quickly on your feet.'

Although Helen would never admit to it, she is clearly happy with what she has achieved. Her garden is absolutely stunning. But when pressed for an assessment she tends to be

FAR LEFT The blue border contains *Cornus controversa* 'Variegata', *Galega* (commonly known as goat's rue) and *Buddleia* 'Nanho blue'.

ABOVE The red border combines the clashing crimsons of roses 'Trumpeter', 'Orange Triumph', 'Bengal Crimson' and 'Frensham'.

quite critical. She admits that the garden can suffer from lack of light due to its enclosure by other buildings, but she offsets this by using a number of cream-coloured variegated plants in her schemes. 'They act in a luminous way in the gloom.' Certainly a splendid specimen of *Cornus controversa* 'Variegata' at the front of the garden, at its best around Easter, gives a much-needed highlight on a dreary day. *Elaeagnus* 'Quicksilver' does likewise with its silver foliage. In spring Helen grows a lot of bulbs for early colour, including snowdrops, followed by narcissi and tulips. Wood anemones, trilliums, and hellebores abound.

'After the camassias are out in late spring there is a pause in the garden,' says Helen, 'but not for long'. An exquisite array of early summer-flowering herbaceous plants follow; *Iris kerneriana*, *Astelia nervosa* and corydalis. Solomon's seals

of all kinds are favourites, as is the double form of *Meconopsis cambrica* which has a long-flowering season. She gets excited about a glossy leafed puya whose colour is like the eye of a peacock's tail feather. In fact her excitement about the whole garden is infectious, and on every visit she has drawn my attention to something new. She is fond of self-seeders like aquilegias which are plentiful; opium poppies, iberis and *Campanula persicifolia*. Helen spices her advice with strange asides, for instance when she suddenly thinks of the poached egg plant *Limnanthes douglasii* she says, 'David Douglas introduced that from North America; did you know he died in a trap for wild animals?' And then as we turn to walk on, an extraordinary fern catches her eye in the cool shady border at the end of the garden. Helen muses on the name '*Athyrium filix-femina* 'Caput Medusae', she says slowly, 'I love that.'

FAR LEFT A wild
gladiolus which
Christopher Lloyd fell in
love with when he visited
Helen's garden.

LEFT *Scabious* 'Chile
Black' with its red-brown
pin-cushion flower head
growing in the red border.

My own special favourites are her pea tree *Caragana arborescens* 'Lorbergii', a beautiful specimen with grey-green silky bark, elegant pea-like leaves and clusters of yellow flowers in spring. The tree has been pruned to expose its splendid bark and to allow planting at its foot. *Cornus mas* 'Variegata' has similarly been pruned for underplanting, but Helen warns that not all trees allow this treatment.

The alpine gardens, where plants are grown in gravel covered keyhole-shaped raised beds, are full of treasures. They include the Plymouth strawberry, named by Tradescant in the seventeenth century, and *Boenninghausenia abliflora*, a member of the rue family. 'I found it growing in the hills of Nepal. You just have to grow something with a name like that!'

Moving back to her house past the whorls of blue *Plectranthus argentatus* in pots, Helen admits that even famous gardeners can let their imagination get the better of their practical side: 'Someone gave me a *Rosa banksii* last week and I woke up in the middle of the night thinking "Marvellous, I will put it in a pot and let it scramble over the flat roof and down the back of the house". When I came out in the morning I realised that the roof was pitched…'

LEFT Tall pyramids of Rodgersia, red leafed spiky cordyline and the New Zealand daisy celmisias are planted below a paper-bark maple *Acer griseum*.

RIGHT *Dierama pulcherrimum* 'Blackbird' (commonly called Angels' Fishing Rods) grow well in Ireland, thriving on the rich soil and moist climate.

Michael & Louisa
de las Casas

LARCHILL

AT THE TOP OF THE COCKLESHELL TOWER IN LARCHILL ARCADIAN GARDENS with Michael de las

Casas I couldn't help asking 'Exactly how did you come to be here?' 'Well, we did look inside the

house but not before we had seen all this,' says the owner and restorer of this extraordinary land-

scape, gesturing towards the towers and follies, the lake, the distant Pugin spire in Maynooth and the

towering Wicklow Mountains on the horizon.

Michael and Louisa de las Casas came to Larchill, near Kilcock in Co. Kildare, primarily because it

seemed an agreeable place and big enough to let them pursue their main objective of

raising rare breeds of farm animals, everything from Hebridean Soay sheep to Killorglin Puck goats.

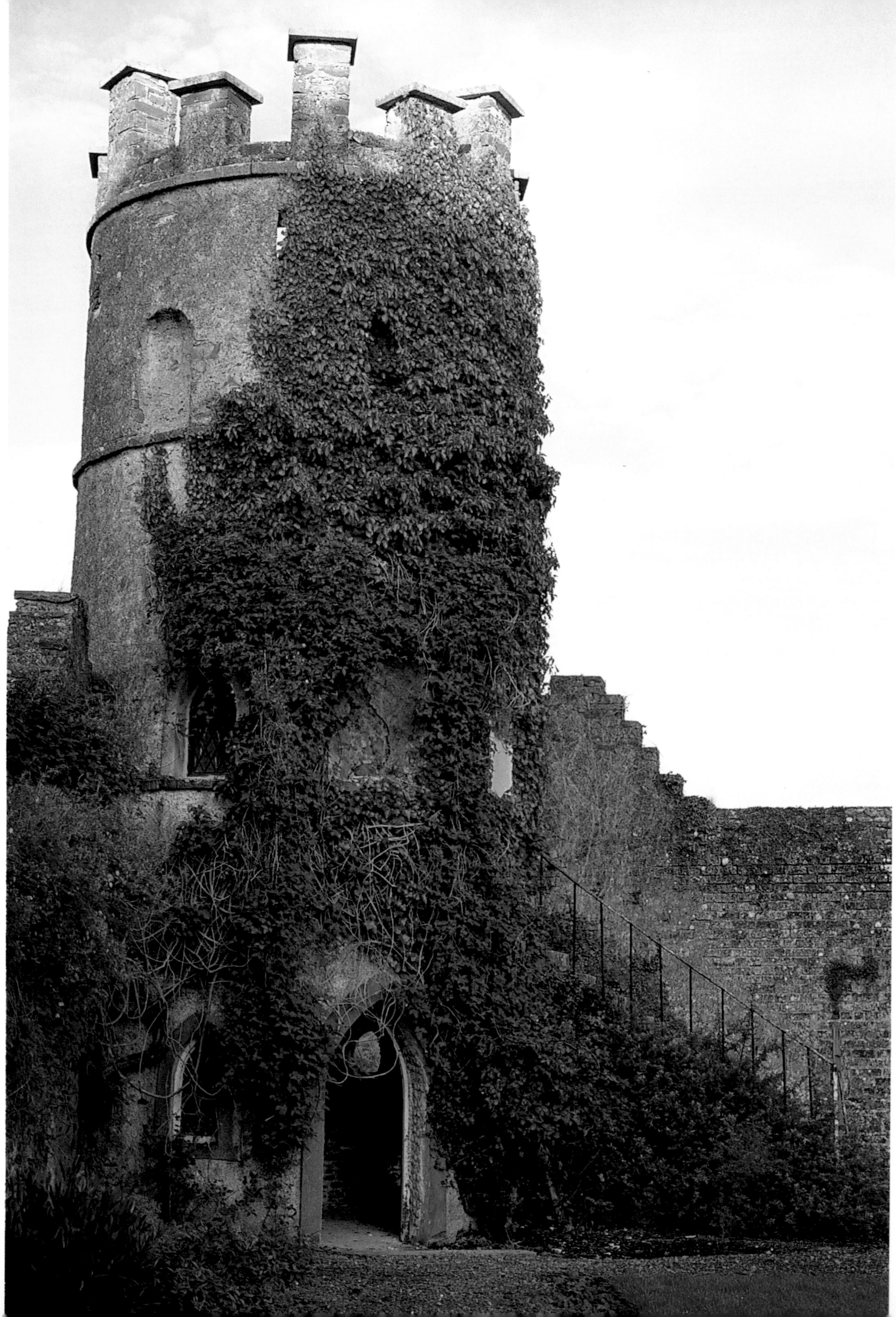

Soon after they bought the 24 hectare (60 acre) property in 1993 they were visited by their friend Paddy Bowe, an architect and garden historian. 'He told us we were the proud new owners of the sole surviving *ferme ornée* (ornamental farm) in Ireland and the British Isles.' It has great horticultural and historical importance.

Fermes ornées were briefly fashionable in the eighteenth century, part of the movement away from the geometric formal style of the previous century towards more natural landscapes. The farms aimed to integrate agriculture and horticulture, combining function and pleasure. Buildings were made attractive, and paths were laid next to hedgerows which were planted with climbers and shrubs. Sometimes herbaceous borders were planted alongside the hedges.

It was probably in the 1740s that the Prentice family of Dublin began to implement the ideas that survive at Larchill today. Once they learnt of its importance, Michael and

A B O V E   Shellwork in the cockle tower, with wrought iron staircase and leaded window.

R I G H T   Behind the house the farmyard contains a menagerie including pot-bellied pigs, goats and fowl.

L E F T   The cockle tower in the walled garden.

P R E V I O U S   L E F T A mock naval fort called 'Gibraltar' sits in the middle of the lake.

P R E V I O U S   R I G H T Michael, Louisa and their children Fenton and Mia.

Louisa decided to carry on the tradition, seeking financial help from the Great Gardens of Ireland Restoration Scheme and the National Heritage Council to bring Larchill back to its original glory.

Today's visitors discover the yard behind the house is alive with every manner of fowl. An Andalucian cockerel marshals his flock of Marrons and Seabright bantams, while a Greylag goose pays no particular attention to the scuttling hens and vociferous cockerel. The stables house a pair of Vietnamese pot-bellied pigs, and a pair of Kerry ponies, a

stallion and mare, share an adjoining yard with a donkey. In a third yard is the headquarters of The Irish Centre for Architectural Conservation and Training, a company offering training in aspects of building and conservation using lime rather than modern cement mortar. They provide essential skills in the restoration of old buildings of the type found at Larchill. This method brings an authentic feel to the work.

The first hint of the follies that await comes when you pass from the yard into the walled garden, through a door under castellated walls. The cockleshell tower, three storeys

high with stained glass windows, stands sentinel in the
southwest corner. The interior walls are set with seashells,
including a beautiful conch shell brought back from the West
Indies by the Watson family who became proprietors of
Larchill after the Prentices.

The walled garden is rectangular and runs from north to
south. The south-facing wall is hollow, allowing it to catch
extra heat to grow tender summer fruits such as peaches and
nectarines; two old figs survive in the corner. Herbaceous
borders have been planted against the walls. The remainder

ABOVE This statue of
Nimrod used to be in the
middle of the lake.

ABOVE RIGHT
Springs feed the eel pond
below the house.

FAR RIGHT 'The
Foxes Earth'. Mr Watson,
a hunting man, worried
he would be reincarnated
as a fox; to save himself
from the hounds he
built this folly for his
protection in a future life.

of this garden is divided into three sections, a fine parterre, a
central section with four beds for herbs, and an area for ornamental gourds. There is also a pond in a semi-orchard area
with an area of grass holding spring bulbs such as snakeshead
fritillaries, cowslips and narcissi. 'Rory's Folly', a rosewalk
pergola (designed and implemented by Michael and Louisa's
head gardener Rory Canavan) divides the garden crossways.

The *ferme ornée* is at its best in the farmyard. Here Michael
has built high-cost housing for his rare breed animals, complete with battlements, towers and Gothic windows, there
are even ground floor flats for the pigs! A two-storey chicken
house has a connecting bridge to another chicken house, and
there is an entire castle for the Killorglin goats who peer
down from the battlements at amazed observers.

From the front of Larchill house the land slopes gently
away over a ha-ha to an enormous lake. From afar what
appear to be the rusting hulks of merchant ships protrude
from the water. Closer inspection reveals an island fort,
known as Gibraltar, and a Greek temple, the twin glories of
Larchill. When Michael and Louisa arrived these were completely overgrown and the lake filled in. Today they gleam in
the light reflected from the lake, and a statue of Bacchus rises
from the water. The temple has a plunge pit within the pond

which collects rainwater for private bathing. The area in and around the lake is a terrific mass of follies. No dates exist for any of them but the lake was here in 1770, and the follies must have followed soon after. A circle of beech trees (a *feuille*, the origin of the word folly) sits on a raised mound, which was probably a viewpoint focusing on the water. Under the feuille is a sunken Gothic boathouse.

Wandering back up towards the house through the mixed herd of 'Kerry Blue' cattle and Jacob sheep you see the Eel Trap folly and then an extraordinary mound with a pillared temple on top, surrounded by castellated stone walls. This is the Foxes Earth. A nineteenth-century owner and Master of Foxhounds became convinced he would be reincarnated as a fox. So he built himself this sanctuary and added a Gothic vault with two hound-proof tunnels going up into the mound. It is worth travelling over continents to see these Larchill follies.

Michael is now chairman of The Great Houses, Castles and Gardens of Ireland Committee. He knows better than anyone the importance of safeguarding the past for the future, and the rescue of Larchill is a tribute to himself and Louisa, their family, and all the workers and donors involved.

KYLEMORE ABBEY

WHEN INDUSTRIALIST MITCHELL HENRY TOOK HIS ULSTER-BORN WIFE MARGARET to Connemara for their honeymoon, she was so captivated by the small hunting lodge at Kylemore, at the feet of the Twelve Pins Mountains between Clifden and Letterfrack, that she expressed a desire to live there. Overtaken by the romance of the place the bridegroom purchased the lodge and its estate in 1862, and built a splendid castle there. This romantic spirit holds a special resonance for me because this is where I first travelled with my husband-to-be, Tom, to see the restoration project in 1997.

FAR LEFT Tom Petherick (second from left), joins restoration workers.

LEFT Kylemore Abbey lies in a landscape of richly coloured hills and still loughs.

BELOW All kinds of lichen thrive here.

NEXT LEFT Clearing and slashing the wilderness before restoration began.

NEXT RIGHT Outlines of the original Victorian flower beds and iron arches before restoration and planting with bedding plants.

Henry's castle was built in 1867. Now known as Kylemore Abbey, it is home to a Benedictine community of nuns and a boarding school. When the building was completed, Henry set about creating a high-walled 2.5 hectare (6 acre) kitchen garden. This scale of garden was at that time unrivalled in Ireland. Behind thick stone and brick walls, he built twenty-one glasshouses and all the accompanying services required for such an undertaking. Herbaceous borders, Victorian bedding schemes, glasshouses of bananas, nectarines, figs and melons, vineries and peach houses were all constructed, along with a tropical house, a palm house and two ferneries. This was a giant enterprise.

For six glorious years Kylemore fulfilled the Henrys' dream. Then tragedy struck. In 1878 Margaret died, and in 1892 their daughter drowned. The estate was auctioned.

It failed to sell immediately but in 1903 Mr Zimmerman of Cincinnati bought it for his daughter, the Duchess of Manchester. She had little interest in the estate which lay empty until it was purchased by the Benedictine nuns in 1920 with the help of public loans.

Since 1975, when it was first tentatively opened to tourists, the community has expanded. There is now a visitor centre and a large restaurant and the long-neglected gardens are being restored. In 1995 the nuns commissioned an archaeological survey of the gardens. Its results, with a number of excellent photographs from the end of the last century, gave a clear picture of the design of the walled garden. A serpentine stream wound north-south down the middle of the garden, crossed at the mid-point by a wide path running

east-west. The four sections contained the glasshouse complex and beds for cut flowers on the eastern side, trees and shrubs, with fruit and vegetables to the west.

Before the start of the restoration programme, only the foundations of the glasshouses and the bare shape of parterres in front of them were visible. Two huge cordylines looked as though they had escaped from captivity. The serpentine stream still had a bank of lichen-covered elms running down its edge that once provided shelter against the prevailing westerlies. Extensive clearing work since has uncovered much more, both plants and structures. The restoration team is gradually piecing together the remains of what was once a state of the art garden, and it may be working again soon. It was certainly far too interesting to end up in ruins.

DETAILS OF GARDENS OPEN TO THE PUBLIC

Altamont
Co. Carlow
Admission: £3.00
Open: Every Sunday and Bank Holiday – or by appointment 2pm-6pm
Phone: +353 (0) 503-59128
Directions: 5½ miles (9 km) from Tullow on the Tullow Bunclody Road – look for a turning north, follow signs and a classical stone gateway.

Ballymaloe Cookery School
Co. Cork
Admission:£3.00
Open: 1 April-30 September 9am-6pm
Phone: +353 (0) 21-646-785
Directions: Signs in Castlemartyr on the main Waterford Cork Road. Follow road to Ballycotton until you see signs.

Birr Castle
Co. Offaly
Admission: Adults £400; OAPs and Students £3.20; Children £2.50; Families £11; Group rate for groups of twenty and over.
Other: Pre-booked guided tours, £25
Open: Every day throughout the year
9am-6pm
Phone: +353 (0) 509-20336
Directions: Entrance Situated at the end of the Mall in the centre of town.

Butterstream
Co. Meath
Admission: £3.00; Students £2.00; Children £1.00
Open: 1 April-30 September (daily)
11am-6pm
Phone: +353 (0) 46-36017
Direction: Signposted from the centre of Trim.

Creagh
Co. Cork
Admission: Adults £3.00; Children £2.00
Open: 1 March-31 October 10am-6pm

Phone: +353 (0) 28-22121
Directions: On the right, 4 miles (6½ km) outside Skibbereen on the Baltimore road.

Eden Plants
Co. Leitrim
Phone for details of opening times.
Phone: +353 (0) 725-4122

Glenveagh Castle
Co. Donegal
Admission to Gardens only:
Adults £2.00; OAP £1.50; Students and Children £1.00; Groups over twenty £1.50/person; Famies £5.00

Admission to Gardens & tour of the Castle:
Adults £4.00; OAP £3.00; Students and Children £2.00 Groups over twenty £3.00/person; Families £10.00
Other: Guided tours of the gardens at 2pm every Tuesday and Thursday in Summer. No extra charge.
Open: 17 March-30 November 10am-6.30pm (last admission 5pm)
Phone: +353 (0) 74-37088
Directions: about 8 miles (12.8 km) from Churchill on the R251.

Glin Castle
Co. Limerick
Admission to Castle & Gardens: £3.00; Groups of eight and over (by arrangement) £2.00/person
Other: Guided tours of the castle on the half hour. No extra charge.
Open: 1 May-30 June – or by appointment 10am-12 noon and 2pm-4pm
Phone: +353 (0) 683-4112
Directions: 9 miles (14½ km) from Foynes on the N69 to Limmerick.

Helen Dillon
45 Sandford Road, Dublin
Admission: £3.00; OAP £2.00
Open: March, July, Aug (daily)

April, May, June, September (Sundays only)
2pm-6pm
Phone: +353 (0) 1-497-1308
Directions: Situated behind trees in a cul-de-sac by the junction of Malborough and Sandford Road. On the right just after the church.

Kilfane Glen and Waterfall
Co. Kilkenny
Admission: £3.00; Groups by written arrangement
Open: 1 May-30 September 11am-6pm (Tuesday-Friday) 2-6pm (Sundays)
Phone: +353 (0) 56-24558
Directions: Almost 2 miles (3 km) off the Dublin-Waterford Road, 2¼ miles (3½ km) above Thomastown.

Kylemore Abbey
Co. Galway
Admission to Gardens only:
Adults £3; Students and OAPs £2.50; Families £5
Open: Mid March to the end of October
10am-5:30pm
Phone: +353 (0) 954-1146
Directions: In the far west corner of Connemara, between Letterfrack and Leenane on the N59.

Lakeview
Co. Cavan
Open: By appointment only
Phone: +353 (0) 464-2480

Larchill
Co. Kildare
Admission: Adults £3.25; Children £1.50
Open: 1 May-30 September 12pm-6pm
Phone: +353 (0) 162-87354
Directions: From Dublin take the M4, exit at Kilcock, follow the road to Trim until you see signposts to Larchill.

Lodge Park
Co. Kildare
Admission to Garden only: £2.00
Other: Phone for Straffan

Steam Museum details.
Open: June-July (Tuesday-Friday and Sunday)
August (Tuesday-Friday) – or by appointment 2pm-6pm
Phone: +353 (0) 1-628-8412
Directions: Just outside Straffan, turn off the N7 at Kill or off the N4 at Lucan or Maynooth.

Mount Stewart
Co. Down
Admission to House & Gardens:
Adults £3.50; Children £1.75; Groups of fifteen and over, £3.00/person
Other: Guided tours of the house every ½ hour – last tour at 5pm. No extra charge. Free admission to the temple.
Open: May-September (except Tuesdays)
April and October (weekends only)
1pm-6pm

Admission to Temple only:
Adults £1.00; Children 50p

Admission to Gardens only:
Adults £3.00; Children £1.50; Groups of fifteen and over, £2.50/ person
Other: Garden tours arranged by appointment only. Free admission to the temple.
Open: April-October
11am-6pm
Phone: +44 (0) 1247-783-387
Directions: On the east shore of Strangford Lough, 5 miles (8km) south east of Newtownards on the A20 Belfast Portaferry Road.

Spinners Town House
Co. Offaly
Open: All year for Bed and Breakfast and to view the garden.
Phone: +353 (0) 509-21673
Directions: Located in Castle Street, opposite Birr Castle walls, below the main entrance.

INDEX

Page numbers in *italics* refer to illustrations; those in **bold** refer to significant collections

AUTHOR'S ACKNOWLEDGEMENTS

It all began with a grant from Valerie Finns and the Merlin Trust. I can't thank her enough, for sending me to photograph Irish gardens in 1995. Her introduction for gardeners such as Jim Reynolds, Helen Dillon and the Shackleton family began my love affair with all things Irish, especially the gardens.

Thanks go to Jim Reynolds for being a true friend all the way along me to 'get a grip' after I voiced misgivings over the task ahead, the project may never have got off the ground. Helen Dillon offered countless practical advice and support and her garden never failed to inspire me. The Shackleton family accommodated me and my travelling companions on the first trip – the resulting photographs of Beech Park later became an article for Gardens Illustrated. I am thrilled to included Daphne's wonderful new garden at Lakeview. Timmy and Darina Allen have been enthusiastic throughout and are like family. I couldn't go to Cork without rushing in to visit and Timmy did the honour of giving me away at my wedding. Nick and Susan Mosse helped me to plan the book and organised for me to fly home early after one disastrous trip when it rained constantly. Corona North and Colm McElwee at Altamont provided inspiration for the book and helped in the first stages of development. Martin Sherry and Ken Lambert from Creagh kindly took me to the Irish Gardens Conference in Crom Castle in 1997 and rescued me from a terrible car accident near Naas the same year. Maureen Barfoot and her intrepid gardening friends Yvonne, Clare and Janie Metcalfe gave me a huge welcome in Northern Ireland and introduced me to David Stewart-Moore, in North Antrim. Seán Ó'Gaoithín showed me a way of gardening that is rare to find as did Daphne Shackleton. Sean O'Criadain was incredibly kind to allow me to photograph his fiercely protected secret garden in Cork, as were David Stewart-Moore, Keith Lamb and Janie Metcalfe and her husband Brian. Everyone at Kylemore was extremely helpful. Thank you to Desmond and Olda Fitzgerald for allowing me to include Glin Castle and Brendan and Alison Rosse at Birr Castle. Joe and Fiona Breen at Spinners Town House in Birr were great to meet with their exquisite Mediterranean courtyard garden and relaxed generosity. Sarah Guinness was patient and gracious allowing me to come to stay several times, trying to catch some good weather over a miserable wet and windy summer. Mikey and Louisa de las Casas were very entertaining and hospitable at Larchill and I fell in love with their pug dog Rosie. Thanks also to Rod Alston at Eden Plants for allowing me to disturb his busy day and to the National Trust for access to Mount Stewart, climbing on top of the roof to gain an aerial view. Thank you also to Melissa Brooke and Lizzie O'Connell, for their open-hearted hospitality and to Rachel Lamb for helping with contacts. Thanks to my loyal sister, Sarah, for endlessly being at the end of the phone for me.

Thank you to Kyle Cathie for taking the project on and the angelic Kate Oldfield, my editor, for her endless patience and hard work. Thank you to the wonderful Vanessa Courtier for designing the book so beautifully and to Nori and Sandra Pope for recommending her to me.

But most of all I want to thank my husband Tom Petherick, who gave me support and confidence all the way.

First published in Great Britain in 1999 by
Kyle Cathie Limited
20 Vauxhall Bridge Road
London SW1V 2SA

ISBN 1 85626 279 0

Text © 1999 Melanie Eclare
Photography © 1999 Melanie Eclare

Editor Kate Oldfield
Editorial assistant Sheila Boniface
Design Vanessa Courtier
Design assistant Gina Hochstein

Melanie Eclare is hereby identified as the author of this work in accordance with Section 77 of the Copyright, Designs and Patents Act 1988

A CIP catalogue record for this title is available from the British Library

Printed and bound in Singapore by Tien Wah Press